A Hot Glue Gun Mess

Funny Stories, Pretty DIY Projects

WILLIAM MORROW
An Imprint of HarperCollinsPublishers

A HOT GLUE GUN MESS. Copyright © 2015 by Kate Albrecht. All rights reserved. Printed in the United States of America. No part of this book may be used or reproduced in any manner whatsoever without written permission except in the case of brief quotations embodied in critical articles and reviews. For information address HarperCollins Publishers, 195 Broadway, New York, NY 10007.

HarperCollins books may be purchased for educational, business, or sales promotional use. For information please e-mail the Special Markets Department at SPsales@harpercollins.com.

FIRST EDITION

Designed by Kris Tobiassen of Matchbook Digital
Photography by Laura Austin and Taren Maroun

Library of Congress Cataloging-in-Publication Data has been applied for.

ISBN 978-0-06-234661-2

15 16 17 18 19   OV/RRD   10 9 8 7 6 5 4 3 2 1

To Joey,

my cowriter in life, and to all the fans of Mr. Kate who make it possible for me to be a creative weirdo. And to my family and friends for taking me on a journey worth writing about... Don't end a sentence with a preposition. Oops.

WARNING: THIS IS NOT A NORMAL CRAFT BOOK

This book contains personal, inspiring, sad, weird, crazy, downright mad, and hilarious stories that I've mined from my crazy-ass life that will make you LOL and PEE (as in urinate in your pants) in a good way, and show you that your next creative project can be sparked from any life experience. I've burned myself with a glue gun so many fucking times I've lost count . . . of my scars. Do these projects without fear. Failure is totally an option and it might happen, but it could also be an epically beautiful failure. Dare to surprise yourself. Dare to delight in yourself—because, why not!

I think one of the most important things following your blog has done for me is help me to embrace the moment and free my spirit. I am very Type A, and I need a reminder every once in a while that it sometimes takes making a mess to create something beautiful.

—*comment posted on the* Mr. Kate *blog*

Contents

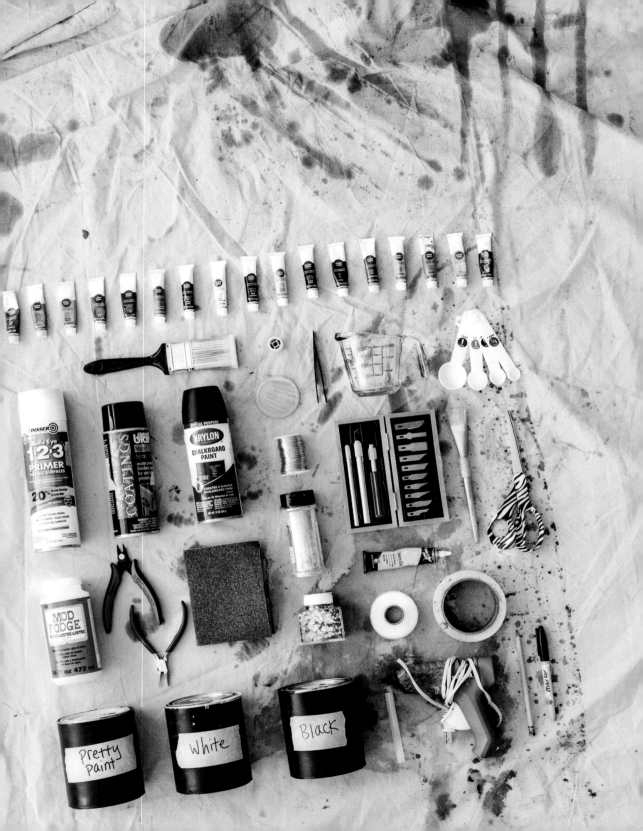

INTRODUCTION: MR. KATE?

My name is Kate, I go by Mr. Kate. And no, I don't have a penis.

Supposedly I didn't cry when I was born. My mom claims I just felt the air with my tiny hands, wiggling them in this new weird world. That was on June 4, 1983, and by now I've gotten my hands into a whole lot of weirdness.

I've built a successful lifestyle and design business around the name Mr. Kate, where I inspire people to think outside the box and create our own unique identities through style and design. I think traditions that don't sit well with you should be challenged and redefined to fit your lifestyle. "Because that's how it's done" doesn't fly with me. . . . I like to *do it myself*, and I apply that philosophy to everything.

The personalities who formed and nurtured me were my oddball, down-to-earth mother, who can make anything from a hand-sewn gown to custom furniture and is more into flannel than diamonds; my grandmother, a champion thrift-store shopper; and my father, who grew his career from struggling comedian to one of the most powerful people in Hollywood. The by-product of his success—money—became the gas that fueled a wildfire of craziness in my childhood, but amid the dysfunction of Hollywood, I've managed to separate myself from the penis cars and facelifts to define my own wacky life.

Vintage found objects—my passion—and my own artwork decorate my walls, and my love of thrift stores and DIY projects helps fill my closet. I have a laugh- and love-filled relationship with my former boy-bander, hot-ass soul mate and business partner, Joey. My life is by no means perfect and it's often messy, but armed with a glue gun, it's uniquely mine.

My yins and yangs are humor and intense ambition, prettiness and roughness, weird and real, rhinestones and dirt, feminine and masculine, Mr. and Kate.

Come with me on a romp through life's follies while wearing fabulous shoes, and celebrate your inner weirdness. Not the bad kind of weirdness—the best kind! The kind that makes you giggle with joy or take in a quick breath of delight. The feeling you get when you put together an outfit that makes you feel so "you" or see a room design that makes you gasp with wonder and say, "I want to live there!" It's about making and *doing* and cultivating your artistic expression inspired by the beautiful details in this outlandish thing we call life.

Because . . . #WhyNot.

Chapter 1
CULT OF THE CARBOHYDRATE

Around the age of fifteen, my tummy had gone from prepubescent flat to looking like it had the slightest layer of padding, filling me out a nearly imperceptible amount. I showed my mom my stomach. "I feel like I might be getting fat," I informed her, looking in the mirror and evaluating myself.

She waved off my concern. "It's adipose tissue," she assured me, always a vocabulary snob. "Everyone stores a little extra fat after puberty. It's normal!"

"Normal" was becoming a foreign concept within our household, with my parents' marriage hitting rock bottom. Our home life was tense, and I was always put in the middle of their arguments. I was like Switzerland, although my new post-puberty chunk was making me feel like the entire European continent. My parents would communicate to me and through me, but not to each other.

"You can eat all the bacon you want," my dad said, explaining the Atkins diet to me. "Carbohydrates are the real demon!"

In the midst of a midlife crisis, my dad had doubled down on his efforts to get rid of his slight paunch of a belly by exercising aggressively and increasing his intake of red meat. He held his wife and teenage daughter to his new standards of fitness.

"So you only eat meat?" I asked my dad, suddenly starting to analyze my teenage eating habits, which were whole and balanced, thanks to my mom's healthy home-cooked meals. But I guess the carbohydrate doesn't fall far from the tree, because his intensity and focus made sense to me, and I was entranced.

"Not just meat—you can eat dairy and vegetables," my dad said, apparently wanting a partner in this diet adventure he was about to tear his canines into.

"What's wrong with bread and fruit?" I asked, aghast. "No pasta?"

"Nope." He shook his head resolutely. "They all make you fat."

With that one remark, I joined the ranks of other tortured souls on this lifelong, miserable path that is being obsessed with what you eat. I became consumed with counting carbohydrates, eating bacon, and, in general, not eating.

My new diet consisted of:

Breakfast: Black coffee and bacon
Mid-morning snack: Diet Coke
Lunch: A couple of bites of chicken breast and more Diet Coke
Afternoon snack: Coffee
Dinner: A few bites of steak and a tiny salad (no dressing!)
Late night snack: A spoonful of sugar-free Cool Whip

My mom was beside herself, furious that my dad had usurped her and was now dictating my eating plan.

"You're losing your cute butt," she said, analyzing my quickly shrinking frame after I had declined her offer of brown rice stir-fry, which I used to love. "Your cheeks look gaunt," she said, shaking her head. "Don't get obsessed, Kate!"

Too late. I was the thinnest I'd been in my teenage years, and my dad kept telling me I looked "great!"

Ironically, I had done an oral report on eating disorders in the eighth grade and had visited a treatment clinic to interview one of the counselors. I was actually very well informed about what I was doing psychologically with my "Miraculous Disappearance of Kate" project. I knew that I had become obsessed with food and my appearance in the mirror because they were the only things I could control in my crumbling family life. I knew this, but it didn't make me stop.

The annoying thing about not eating is, you get hungry.

My severe calorie restriction worked for a couple of months, and then I started binge eating. I would not eat all day and then come home and have an entire tub of Cool Whip up in my room, or my favorite, decaf coffee with whole milk and dark chocolate Milano cookies.

One night, I drank five cups of coffee and ate two entire bags of Milano cookies. I felt so bad about myself that I decided I had to barf it up. I remembered my research for my oral report; I'd learned that some girls gagged themselves with their toothbrush to make themselves throw up.

I went into my bathroom and tried jamming my giant Sonicare electric toothbrush down my throat. It didn't work. My throat was raw. Then I remembered that some bulimic girls used laxatives instead of making themselves throw up. This sounded way better to me than barfing, so I rooted through the medicine cabinet in my parents' bathroom and found a bottle of Philips' Milk of Magnesia. The dosage on the bottle was 1 to 3 teaspoons to relieve constipation, but I wanted extra-quick results, so I chugged half the bottle.

What came next can only be described as hell. My tiny stomach, full of acidic coffee and sugary Milanos, was attacked by this milk of death. Rather than making me poo, it gave me the most intense cramps. I was doubled over in pain but couldn't go to my mom because she'd demand to know how I'd gotten myself into this mess and blame it on my dad.

That day, I learned that laxatives, taken in bulk swigs after eating two whole bags of Milano cookies, don't make you poo—they make you throw up, violently.

I guess I got what I'd hoped for, but the whole experience was beyond traumatizing, for me *and* my toothbrush. I started to cry, glaring at my tear-stained reflection in the mirror, and went to find the only person I thought I could confide in: my crabby grandma, who was visiting us at the time.

I sat her down and confessed my sins. She patted me on the back, cussed out my parents for putting me through too much stress, and made me a comforting bowl of pasta.

It took me a few years of fluctuating weight and weird eating before I decided to look in the mirror and get really real with myself.

"Kate," I said, staring at my naked reflection. "Pay attention! You're not fat, you're short. Boys tend to like you, but you don't like yourself. Working out is good for you—it will save you from a heart attack later, so you should keep doing that—but this whole eating thing has to get under control. Stop obsessing, and please acknowledge that you're not a supermodel and never will be. Your body wants to have some adipose tissue on your tummy and some cellulite on the backs of your upper thighs, and will never let go of that little bulge between your armpit and boob that puffs out *just so* when you're wearing a tank top and bugs the shit out of you. This is your reality, now go love yourself."

Easier said than done, but currently I'm at ease with my body, I don't eat bacon, and I can't even look at a fucking Milano cookie.

DIY Mercury Glass Coffee Table

PREP IT

Glass-topped coffee table (make sure the glass can be separated from the base)—I found mine at the thrift store

Drop cloth

3 cans Krylon Looking Glass spray paint

Spray bottle, filled with half water and half white vinegar

Paper towels

DO IT!

1. Remove the glass top from the coffee table. Lay the glass on the drop cloth with the underside facing up. Spray a layer of the Looking Glass paint evenly over the glass and let it dry (it will take only a few minutes).

2. Spray the vinegar-and-water mixture over the spray-painted glass. Use a paper towel to blot and wipe up the drops of vinegar-water. Tip: When blotting, vary your rubbing pressure to leave more or less paint in areas for a natural look.

3. Repeat steps 1 and 2 with multiple coats of spray paint and blotted vinegar water until you have your desired aged effect. I used five coats of spray paint.

4. Flip your glass over and place it back on the table base so the painted area is on the underside. This will give it that mercury glass effect and protect your paint from wear and tear.

DO IT Elsewhere! Create a mercury glass vase by using the same technique on the inside of a clear vase. Make sure the paint is fully cured before you add water for your flowers.

Chapter 2

HOOKER WITH A HEAD OF GOLD

My early twenties were a mess. My best friend was a high-priced hooker. She was introduced to me as twenty-six-year-old Alex, who worked in fashion. I didn't know her true profession until after our friendship ended years later, when I found out she also had a fake name and was six years older than she claimed. Alex was lovely—funny and charming, with a laid-back beauty—and we would laugh nonstop together.

Alex had this amazing laugh—a loud and genuine cackle. It was the laugh of a girl who didn't give a shit what people thought of her. Her signature look was her long blond hair, which she wore in messy, beachy waves. She drove a Mercedes and had a realistic-looking boob job and lithe friends, which should have raised a red flag to her actual profession, but to naive, twenty-year-old me, she was an intriguing and fantastic friend. At the time, I was acting (a.k.a. auditioning once in a while) and living in Los Angeles while also making my way through undergrad as a part-time film production student. My flexible schedule allowed me to accompany Alex, who split her time between New York and Chicago, on some of her various adventures around the country. She told me that her apartments, fancy cars, racks of designer clothes, and frequent stays at the Four Seasons were funded by an inheritance from her wealthy grandfather. Being a well-off girl from the land of La La and subsidized children, I didn't think twice. I was happy to eat lemon ricotta pancakes and indulge in the beautiful dream that was her life.

My adventures with Alex brought me to places I'd never been before, like Mallorca, Spain, and the time we went to St. Thomas to celebrate my twenty-first birthday. One adventure found us in Arizona staying at Canyon Ranch, a health retreat where you take workout classes all day, eat vegetables, and wear your hair in messy buns. Alex and I took to bribing the waitstaff for larger portions and smuggling coveted oranges to our room for late-night bingeing (I know, it's a sorry excuse for a late-night snack but when you're starving in the desert, in a $1,000-per-night resort, shit is tough). Everything we did was hilarious; we could get the giggles anywhere, especially in an interpretive dance class taught by a man in a loincloth. Alex and I would laugh so hard we couldn't look at each other for fear of a laugh-induced (and calorie-reduced) heart attack. (She also let me feel her saline boob implants, to see what they felt like—they felt pretty real, although I was dissuaded from getting my own by the odd ripples that appeared when she leaned forward—that, and the fact that I'm a pint-size human and adding to my body in any horizontal direction is a "no, thank you!")

On one trip to visit Alex in Manhattan, she told me her "friend" Frank wanted to have lunch with us and then treat us to a massage.

"Wait, what?" I asked "Like, how is this going to work?"

Alex threw back her messy tresses, laughed a big open-mouthed guffaw, and said, "Trust me, I know it sounds creepy, but he's totally harmless. He loves my company because I make him laugh, and I know he'll love you because you're hilarious. He's married! All we have to do is go get a yummy lunch with him and then go up to his giant suite and get massages by professional massage therapists. We can even have our own room!"

I looked skeptical for a second, but then realized that the restaurant served one of my fave Crab Louie salads, and who was I to say no to an hour-long, full-body massage?! So, trusting Alex and her twinkling green eyes and golden locks, I set off with her to our (creepy) lunch.

Frank was already sitting in the plush booth when we got there. He was about sixty, a portly man wearing a giant brown leather blazer-like jacket and black sunglasses. He didn't remove his sunglasses the entire time we had lunch, even though we were inside—gross—and although he was friendly, I wondered what he was hiding under those Foster Grants. Alex and I entertained him with stories of our adventures and my sarcastic commentary on life's problems, such as Alex's tendency to buy two of every designer piece of clothing that she liked and my plans to use the discarded doubles to make a quilt from that she could use on her $20,000 mattress. My rapid-fire conversation was less about impressing him and more to cover my nervousness about the impending rubdown. *What if he gets naked but leaves his sunglasses on!?* I wondered. I shuddered at the thought of his overly tan belly all greased up with massage oil. But I bravely giggled as Alex cackled and Frank polished off an entire steak.

After Frank paid the bill, it was time to head up to the hotel suite that he had gotten specifically for our massages. I was trying to remember if I actually knew any jujitsu moves, in case I had to go all Jackie Chan on his naked old ass. I could taste the Thousand Island dressing rising up my throat.

Would you believe that nothing weird happened? I mean, beyond the creepiness that this old married dude wanted to pay for two full-body massages for us. I hate to end this story without a big finale, but the truth is, when we got up to the hotel room, there were three white-uniformed masseuses—excuse me, massage therapists—two in the bedroom for Alex and me and one set up in the living room for Frank. Alex and I got undressed in the closed room, hopped up on our massage tables, and had a delightful—and very professional—massage from Rosie and Stella, while Frank got his quietly in the other room! It all seemed suspiciously okay, and in hindsight, I'm not sure that all of Alex's "clients" wanted sex. Maybe some of them have a fetish for expensive, professional massages and just want her company. I don't know, I'm not a high-priced hooker!

After Frank paid for the massages, he hugged us good-bye and told us to order room service and charge it to the room. We did just that, and hung out in our hotel robes, relaxing and smelling of massage oil and comped indulgence.

#WhyNot **Hooker or not, I must say Alex always had those perfectly messy waves. Save the saline boobs and flaunt your natural texture with this DIY Beachy Waves Spray to give yourself hair worthy of a high-priced hooker!**

DIY Beachy Waves Spray

PREP IT

1 tablespoon Epsom salts

½ teaspoon coconut extract
(find it at the grocery store—
it smells amazing!)

1 teaspoon argan oil

1 cup warm water

Measuring cup

Measuring spoons

Spray bottle

DO IT!

1. Mix the Epsom salts, coconut extract, argan oil, and warm water together in the measuring cup and pour the mixture into the spray bottle.

2. Spray on damp hair and scrunch with your hands in an upward motion, creating tousled waves and enhancing your natural, messy texture. Let your hair dry naturally or blow-dry with a diffuser.

Chapter 3
IT SMELLS LIKE RAISINS

I got my period in art class. I was twelve years old and my verbose mother had already given me the "birds and bees" talk and alerted me to the impending crimson wave. I knew Aunt Flo was coming.

Earlier that year, I had been jealous of my sixth-grade classmate who had gotten her period. She bragged to a group of girls at school that she had started that morning. She got in trouble for continuing to talk about it during class. The teacher moved her to a seat in the back corner of the classroom, which happened to be close enough to my seat that she could keep saying "the oil is leaking" every few minutes and throw me a knowing glance. I felt left out and wanted some oil to leak out of me!

I spent that summer, as I spent most of my summers, at a little beach house my parents rented in Malibu. It sounds glamorous, but it was kind of a shack of a house. The outside was a gorgeous swath of California coast filled with celebrity neighbors.

My mom had enrolled me in a summer art class down the street, where we were taught the art of chalk pastels. The teacher claimed that true black did not exist in nature, so I was forced to use every other color to make the dark spots on my leopard drawing. It was frustrating, but in the end, it gave depth to my drawing that would probably have not been there if I had been able to use a black pastel.

It was in this class, while trying to create black, that I created brown in my panties.

My stomach had been hurting me, so I went into the bathroom, worried that I was going to have diarrhea in a public restroom. As a general rule, I *do not* go number two in public bathrooms. Fearful that I might have to break this rule to relieve my cramping, I sat down on the toilet, only to discover, to my horror, a very found-in-nature shade of brownish red staining my Tuesday underwear. I was mortified at first because I thought I'd crapped my pants. But then I paused and thought, *Maybe I'm leaking oil!* Not yet knowing the folded-toilet-paper trick, I pulled my pants back up and went out to finish my art class with my legs tightly squeezed together. I didn't want to leak on my chair!

My nanny picked me up from class. Tanya was a twenty-two-year-old blonde with big boobs. I didn't feel close enough to her to tell her that I may or may not have started my period. I rode home smelling the salt air through the open window and discreetly massaging my cramping belly.

Back at the beach house, I found my mother and pulled her into the bathroom.

"Momma," I said, "I think I might have started my period . . . or pooped my pants."

"Oh!" my mom exclaimed excitedly. "I'm so proud of you! Does it smell like raisins?"

I looked at her, disgusted.

"What?" I said quietly, fearful that Tanya could hear our conversation.

"Smell your panties. Period blood smells sweet, like raisins. That's how you'll know for sure."

Holy ugh, my mother had never told me to smell any naturally occurring brownish stuff before. But I had to know for sure if I had just become a woman.

"Okay, get out of here and I'll see what it smells like," I said, pushing my mom out of the bathroom. I proceeded to sniff my panties, and sure enough, it smelled kind of like raisins! Not at all offensive, but a mild, warm, sweet smell.

Upon hearing the final verdict, my mom celebrated with another hug and asked if she could tell my dad when he got home from work. I told her she could, but *not* around me and to not make a big deal out of it. I wanted a toned-down first oil leaking, no public celebrating allowed.

The next couple of days, I busied myself with figuring out how to cram a maxi pad into my bathing suit—tampons were way too scary still, but I wanted to enjoy the ocean. My dad hadn't said anything to me, but two days after Raisin Gate, he took me out to a nice restaurant, just the two of us. After we were done with our meal, he gave me a large black velvet jewelry box and told me to open it.

Nestled inside was a beautiful strand of white sea pearls. My dad told me that "just like a beautiful pearl," I had blossomed into a woman, and he was proud of me.

I was embarrassed but touched, and I'm sure I turned a very found-in-nature shade of pink.

#WhyNot **Celebrate the colorful stains of life with these gorgeous DIY Watercolor Curtains.**

DIY Watercolor Curtains

PREP IT

Measuring tape

Silk fabric, enough to cover your windows plus a couple inches

Iron-on hem tape

Iron and ironing board

Plastic drop cloth

Watercolor paint in the color(s) of your choice

Artist's palette or small cups

Medium to large artist's paintbrush

Curtain rod

Curtain rings with clips

DO IT!

1. Measure your windows with the measuring tape and cut the silk fabric in panels to fit, leaving an extra inch for a hem on the bottom.

2. Hem the bottom of each panel by folding an inch of fabric around a piece of iron-on hem tape and ironing to seal with the iron on a low heat setting. Tip: Use a damp cloth between the iron and silk to help the hem tape bond faster.

3. Lay the silk flat on a drop cloth or in an area you don't mind getting painty. Prep your watercolors by squirting a bit of each color on the palette and mixing with water.

4. Paint your curtains with patches of color, letting the brushstrokes and paint run organically. Use more or less water to intensify the pigment and spread the color. Tip: Experiment with different strokes and techniques, knowing that there's no wrong way to paint these curtains! Let dry thoroughly.

5. To hang your watercolor curtains, attach the unhemmed end of each panel to the clip rings and slide the rings onto the curtain rod. The raw edge allows for more flexibility when hanging if you need to adjust the length.

DO IT Elsewhere! Create wearable art by watercolor painting a thrifted silk blouse! Just make sure to dry clean only!

Chapter 4

PARTY SHOES

When I was little, I used to call my patent leather, Mary Jane–style shoes that had various rhinestone or ruffle embellishments on the toes "party shoes." My party shoe addiction totally raged from age two to age five. My daily ensemble would usually involve a short frilly dress, in ivory or pink, although I wouldn't throw a cherry red or turquoise out of bed, either. The frilly skirt would give way to some lace tights or, on hot days, socks with ruffles. Then came the party shoes, always matching perfectly, of course, to complete the cupcake-topper look that would have made Liberace jizz in his cape.

My mom would attempt to lay out an outfit for me, only to have my discerning toddler self waddle over, give it the once-over, and head back to the closet to start fresh. My parents eventually ceded full control over what I wore to me, which evolved in my teen years to vinyl pants, feather boas, Kool-Aid-dyed hair, blue lipstick, and booty shorts. The one purchase from my parents that I totally approved of was a cha-cha dress they bought for me in the Mexican part of Downtown LA. That thing was the tits! It had more ruffles than Louis the Fourteenth's codpiece and flared out like you wouldn't believe.

No outfit is complete without a good pair of party shoes, and to this day I believe that whatever shoes make you want to party should be the ones you wear every day! My tiny patent leather Mary Janes took me to fifth birthday soirees, then gave way to neon Converse high-tops that took me to awkward mall hangouts. Soon came patent leather Doc Martens, towering platforms (to which I'm still addicted), and underage drinking. Nowadays I spend my time in anything from vintage boots to animal-print wedges, the gaudy shoes my husband, Joey, gives me (which I can't *not* wear) to the occasional designer heels, all of which I never throw away, leaving my closet looking like a drag queen's version of *Hoarders*.

One time, I put my party shoes through someone's windshield. I was in eighth grade and we were piling into my friend James's dad's station wagon to go hang out at his "party house" after school. James had an older brother in high school, which meant hanging at his house allowed us to bum cigarettes and flirt with his older brother's friends.

My party shoes that day were a pair of kelly green Doc Martens with steel toes. Against my mother's rules, I decided it was okay to share the front passenger seat with James. I was trying to cram my junior-high-size butt (not large, mind you) into the bucket seat next to him by using my foot on the front windshield as leverage . . . you know, genius-style.

Well, what do you know? Suddenly there was a popping sound, and a large crack extended from where my steel toe had come in contact with the glass. It was quite beautiful, actually, the shimmery, weblike glass wound, but my momentary aesthetic distraction gave way to horror when I realized I'd created a three-foot-long crack across the entire windshield! James had been facing our other friends packed into the backseat and turned around just after the veins had spread like the crack on a dangerous icy pond. He looked in horror at it, then at me. Immediately tapping into acting roots I knew I had (my mom was in commercials in the seventies, you know), I quickly tucked my short leg down under the dashboard.

"You totally just broke the windshield!" James yelled.

"What?" I exclaimed. "That crack? No, that was there when I got in," I lied. "I saw it!"

Disgusted, James shook his head as his dad opened the driver's side door and sat down behind the wheel. James looked really worried as he asked his dad if the crack had been there before.

His dad frowned and peered at it. "No, definitely don't remember that being there. What happened?" he asked as he looked skeptically at both of us. I was about ready to nervous-pee all over our shared seat. James looked at me expectantly and I knew it was time to . . . keep lying.

"I swear I saw that crack when I got in. It specifically caught my eye because I was going to ask James if someone threw a rock at your car or something?"

The rest of our friends were silent, that kind of awkward silence when you know someone is lying but everyone is too nice to call you out on it. James's dad peered quizzically at my chunky green shoes and sighed.

"Hmm, maybe it was a rock. I didn't realize I had enemies in these parts. Guess I need a new windshield," he said, starting the car and taking us on our merry way.

I found out later that it cost $300 to replace the windshield. I heard James's older brother telling his friend while we smoked cigarettes by his dirty pool. *Yikes!* I thought, as I puffed on my American Spirit. *That's, like, the price of a* reaallly *nice pair of shoes!*

#WhyNot **Whether your shoes are going to a party or through a windshield, they should be worth a celebration. If you can't Louboutin, then LIEboutin and create your own pair of these DIY Metal-Embellished Shoes—Two Ways.**

DIY Metal-Embellished Shoes—Two Ways

Studded-Heel Boots

PREP IT

Flat-backed pyramid studs

Heeled boots

Strong glue, like E6000 or 3M Scotch Super Strength Adhesive

DO IT!

1. Decide how you want to arrange the studs on the heels of your boots, keeping in mind that the curve of the heel may cause spacing issues. I chose to fill the gaps on the back of my heel by turning the square studs to diamond orientation.

2. Use a small amount of the strong glue to carefully adhere the studs to your shoes. I chose to make tiny glue dots along the heel and then place the stud over the glue. If needed, use a little tape to hold the studs in place as the glue dries. Tip: Glue studs to one side of the heel at a time and let dry before moving on to the other side.

Noodle Bead Sandals

PREP IT

Noodle beads

Strappy sandals

Strong glue, like E6000 or 3M Scotch Super Strength Adhesive

DO IT!

1. Decide where you want to stack your noodle beads to embellish the design of your shoes. Tip: Test to see if your desired placement will work when you're wearing your shoe as well, since that often changes the shape.

2. Use a small amount of the strong glue on the beads, then carefully adhere them to your shoes. If needed, use a little tape to hold the beads in place as the glue dries.

Chapter 5
LADY HUMPALOT

I discovered my love of humping when I was around the age of two. I know, I started young. I realized that if I rocked side to side while straddling something, be it the arm of a couch, a rocking horse, etc., it gave me a wonderful sensation starting in my *pussa*, as my Hispanic nanny called it, and emanated up into my tummy, making me feel so cozy delicious. I remember on one occasion climbing on a houseguest's head to see how that humping experience felt, but I quickly got scooped up by one of my embarrassed parents. That was the only time they stopped me from my humping activities; most of the time they let me do what I apparently needed to do, without bothering me or making me feel guilty. Although I do remember one other time my mom asked me to stop humping while she was reading me my bedtime story because I was shaking the bed too much and she couldn't see the words. The nerve.

Stuffed animals were my very favorite thing to hump. Not just any stuffed animals— they had to be the *perrrrfect* size and shape, and not have big plastic eyes or noses, because who wants that digging into your tummy when you're trying to get off?

I had various love affairs with the chosen stuffed animals I'd flattened to perfection from my incessant mounting. There was Barr, the white teddy bear, whose arms would tuck neatly at his sides for the perfect humping experience. There was also a tiny black Scotty dog that I named Africa. I was totally nondiscriminatory in my sexual partners starting at a very young age.

Humping was how I relaxed myself every night as I fell asleep. I would bury myself under the covers (so no monsters could see me, of course), lay on my tummy, tuck Barr or Africa between my legs, and rock myself to sleep.

The problem was that I had to take my stuffed animals with me on vacation. My mom would cram them into a suitcase, and they would travel to various exotic locations with me. On one trip, when I was eight years old, my parents took me to Europe for a "princess trip." My sister had been born two years prior and was a tiny terror. The three of us escaped to Europe, leaving Terrible Two Tess with my grandma, and we stayed at various chateaus in the mountains of France and Germany. I dressed in tiaras and silk veils and dined in the fanciest restaurants. I was a very well-behaved princess . . . until night fell, when I'd tear it up with Barr in the sixteenth-century castle turret room.

Maybe it was the gods smiting me for my bestiality, because Barr got thrown out with the sheets at one of those castles. I had fallen asleep on Barr and in the morning left his white fuzzy body in the tangled mess of white sheets to eat choc-olate croissants and go out for a day of princess activities. I'd usually return to the room after the housekeepers had visited to see pancake Barr propped on a per-fectly made bed, where he always looked like he was in a daze, probably because he wasn't getting enough oxygen through his smooshed snout. But one day, he wasn't there. My parents called down to the front desk to see if anyone could locate the flat white bear in that day's dirty sheets. But to no avail. Maybe it was the language barrier, or Barr himself begging not to be released back to my loins, but I never saw him again. For the rest of the trip, I had to hump a wad of dirty princess dresses, which was just not the same. Africa suffered the same fate. He got thrown out with the hotel sheets in Hawaii.

I eventually graduated to boyfriends, and the good thing was that by that time, I was a very practiced humper; I knew exactly what I needed to do to get off. Who cares about the dudes? They're easy. Really, ladies, I highly recommend that you find your-self a nice stuffed animal or couch arm or whatever works for you and discover your own pleasure. The O should always be an option. Just make sure your mate doesn't get thrown out with yesterday's dirty sheets. It's such a hassle.

#WhyNot **Celebrate your animal nature! Have a royally good time with these fun DIY Royal Animal Rings.**

DIY Royal Animal Rings

PREP IT

Craft knife

Cutting board

Small plastic animals

Ring bases

Marker

Strong glue, like E6000 or 3M Scotch Super Strength Adhesive

Various metal and rhinestone chains

Various colorful beads

Bead endcaps and cones

Sequins

Small pliers or tweezers

Wire cutters

1. Using a craft knife on a cutting board, cut the heads off your plastic animals, leaving enough neck space to add a necklace later—about the width of a chain is a safe bet.

3. Give your animals fabulous accessories and hats using your chains, beads, and cone beads. The tweezer makes it much easier to place the tiny elements and position the chains in the glue around the base of their heads. Tip: I used the bead cones and endcaps for party hats decorated with colorful beads and sequins. I found it easier to build the hats first with glue and then glue the finished hat on the top of the animal heads.

4. Let the glue dry, then have a party!

2. Slide the ring onto a marker cap to hold the ring upright. Mount the animal heads to the ring bases with strong glue and let dry for around 30 minutes, or until they feel secure.

DO IT Elsewhere! Mount a royal animal on your wall to hold your keys using a large plastic animal and a painted wooden plaque!

Chapter 6
SOUL MATES
ON MOVIE SETS

Living in Hollywood, I caught the acting bug in high school and prepared myself for a glamorous career playing stimulating roles and dating A-list movie hunks. Instead, I spent most days sitting in traffic going from audition to audition and eating on the couch in the evenings with my unemployed boyfriend. The roles I actually booked ranged from popular bitch to dumb slut to über-dork, and even über-über-dumb-slut-dork. I guess my nasal voice and my awkward audition room decorum didn't make me a shoo-in for the intellectual lead.

My latest part was a supporting role as a bitchy cheerleader in an independent film set to shoot in lovely Salt Lake City, Utah. The film centered around two dorky girls who kidnapped their favorite boy band to play for their school and ensure their popularity. The band was to be played by the real-life, current heartthrob boy band The Click Five. My character was the villain out to ruin everyone's lives. While I was less than thrilled about having to wear a short cheerleading skirt in the frigid Salt Lake City winter, there was something fun about the idea of holing up in a hotel for a month with a famous band.

The hotel, which housed all the cast members, quickly became a giant dormitory and playground for everyone's off-set shenanigans. I remember when I first laid eyes on him. His name was Joey, he was the drummer of the band, and he was adorable. He was a good six feet tall, towering over my five-footness. I already knew what Joey looked like from the band's music videos, but he was impossibly dreamier in person. Joey's style was impeccably laid-back rocker, with bell-bottom jeans that fit his butt like woah (I later learned they were girls' jeans, which he wore for their Jagger-like fit). His long, floppy hair fell over one of his gorgeous blue eyes, and his tight T-shirt showed off his drummer arms. Most of our time was spent in the room of Ben, the band's keyboard player, a lovable goofball and musical genius. Ben would write songs, Joey would jokingly rap to them, and I would dance in my yoga pants (usually because I was fresh from the gym, where I was trying to maintain my cheerleader physique). I immediately became a groupie. The only problem was, I had a boyfriend.

To vent my unvanquished sexual tension, I tried to coach one of the other actresses on how to woo the elusive drummer boy, but he opted for the Mormon wardrobe assistant as his on-set romance instead. He confided in me between scenes and we joked about his failure to get past first base with her. I suffered my way through three weeks on location watching Joey gyrate take after take in the school auditorium (his movie character was the bass player, so he'd dance and thrust around the stage) as the blushing wardrobe assistant attended to his every lint-rolling need. At twenty-three years old, I had a classic bout of high school jealousy while playing a high schooler on the set of a high school.

Joey's scenes involved dancing, slapping the bass, and kissing the lead girl. My big scene involved getting my hair set on fire by the bumbling female protagonists in front of the whole school and then put out, take after take, with a prop fire extinguisher filled with whipped cream. I was miserable. I had a bad case of the flu and willed myself through each scene even though I felt near death. To make matters worse, the whipped cream had gone sour from hours inside the fire extinguisher, and I had to choke down vomit every time I was hit by a super-strong spray of rancidity. The whipped cream curdled in my cheerleader hair and dripped down my hoisted-up cleavage. After about thirty takes, the flu and the special effects had taken their toll on me, and tears slid down my cheeks through the caked-on dairy. I was heading back to my trailer, cold and stinking of rotten milk, when I felt a tap on my shoulder, and there was Joey, grinning. His face softened when he saw my misery, and he gave me a hug, even though I smelled like the inside of a college boy's mini fridge. "You're such a good actress, Kate!" he insisted. "I watched every single one of your takes on the monitor, and I was so impressed!"

I sneezed, a glob of whipped cream dripped on his tight vintage T-shirt, he laughed. Joey and I became great friends, my flu went away, and I went back to LA . . . and my boyfriend.

Six months later, I flew to New York City to attend the movie premiere at the Tribeca Film Festival. My time away from our movie-set dorm had put me back on the hamster wheel of failed auditions, and my relationship was continuing in its humdrum status quo. I knew the whole cast, including the band boys, were going to be at the premiere, and I was looking forward to celebrating on the magical isle of Manhattan.

I ran into Joey outside the theater signing autographs for a giant group of fans. He saw me walking up, smiled, and yelled, "Hey, Kate!" He handed back the paper and marker to the googly-eyed tween and gave me a big hug. He looked dashingly sexy in a skinny suit reminiscent of the sixties Beatles style, and his long-armed embrace instantly revived my crush. I knew right then that my boyfriend was as good as dead.

That night there was an after party at a popular club, where Joey and I made our way to the middle of the packed dance floor. What started out as a goofy dance-off turned into an electrically charged bump and grind. The booming hip-hop music faded away, our dancing slowed, and all of a sudden Joey's lips were on mine and I . . . whip creamed in my panties.

We are now married . . . and go jean shopping together.

#WhyNot **Get struck by Cupid's arrows and protect your precious things in this DIY Cupid's Arrows Jewelry Box.**

DIY Cupid's Arrows Jewelry Box

PREP IT

Unfinished wood box

Wood-burning pen

DO IT!

1. Practice the wood-burning technique on the underside of the jewelry box (or a similar piece of scrap wood) so that you begin to get a feel for how it works and how hard to press the pen tip. Tip: You may want to sketch your arrows on your box top using a pencil before you start burning.

2. Burn the arrows into the wood on the top and/or sides of the box. Follow the diagram to help you get the hang of drawing a basic arrow shape and then get creative with the embellishments, like striped feathers and multiple lines to mimic rawhide wrapped around the arrowhead and shaft.

DO IT Elsewhere! Wood-burn an entire unfinished wood chair for a rustic statement piece!

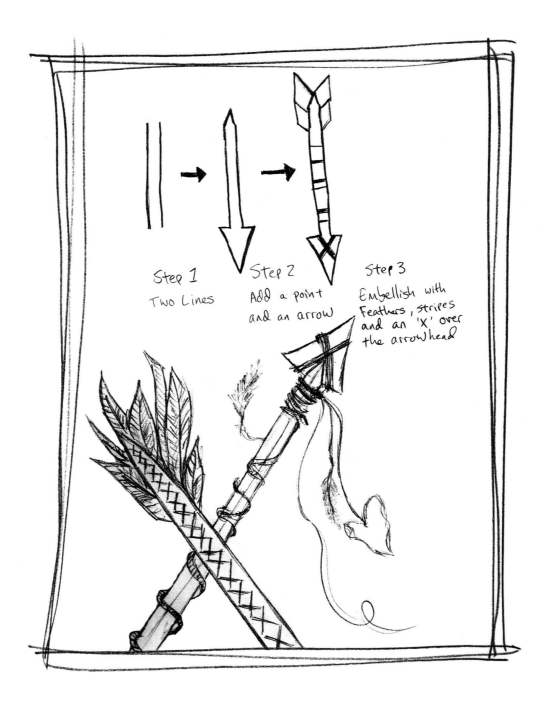

Step 1

Two Lines

Step 2

Add a point
and an arrow

Step 3

Embellish with
Feathers, stripes
and an 'X' over
the arrowhead

Chapter 7

PRELUDE TO THE PREPUBESCENT

Peter the pedophile piano teacher plunked his plump pinkies playing "Prelude to the Prepubescent."

Mr. Peter Brown was my piano teacher from third to sixth grade. We'd tickle the ivories during private lessons in the music room at school every Tuesday at 3:30 P.M., until he was caught in a sting operation with child pornography.

I was never very musically inclined, but my artsy school required me to play various instruments throughout the years. During my illustrious elementary career, I butchered the recorder, violin, piano, and alto saxophone. Mr. Brown was an assistant to our orchestra teacher and made extra cash teaching private lessons to students after school. My parents wanted to improve my musical abilities, so I became a regular under Mr. Brown's tutelage.

I dreaded our one-on-one afternoon sessions, mostly because I never practiced and Mr. Brown's breath smelled repugnantly like ham. Mr. Brown had a ponytail, one caterpillar eyebrow across his entire forehead, a rotund belly, chubby fingers, and what I assumed (by the audible nose wheezing) was a deviated septum.

Twice a year, Mr. Brown's breathing intensified as he busied himself getting prepped for the recital in which we all had to perform to show off our progress. My stress mounted as the dreaded recital drew near. His eyebrow waggled as I lamented my inability to get past *Bastien Piano Basics 1*.

"But I'm really good at 'Heart and Soul'!" I insisted, wide eyed.

He relented and said I could play "Heart and Soul" at the upcoming recital, but only if I convinced my friends Riya and Missy to play a foursome arrangement with him.

Done! I thought. *This is so perfect, because I already know how to play "Heart and Soul" like whoa—Riya and Missy and I play it all the time for fun!* Thus, our after-school sessions turned into fun hangouts with me and my girlfriends playing a round robin of "Heart and Soul" with Mr. Brown. We would all sit on the piano bench together, three tiny prepubescent girl butts next to one sweaty lard ass. Each of us would play a portion of "Heart and Soul" at different octaves and complexities before the person at the high end of the piano would stand up and walk to the bass end to take over the part from the person next to her (or him). It was interactive and fun and we *all* loved it.

Our rendition of a song easy enough to play with your feet earned us the only standing ovation at the recital. The kids who spent hours practicing Bach preludes scoffed in bewilderment.

When in fifth grade, it was time for me to pick a wind instrument. My dad really wanted me to play his childhood alto sax, which was aging nicely in the garage. Fine, whatever, it was nearly as big as I was but at least it was shiny and kind of gold colored. In their infinite parental wisdom, they signed me up for additional private sax lessons with Mr. Brown.

My hour-long piano lessons next to his sweaty belly led to my hour-long saxophone lessons, where we'd sit on folding chairs sucking on reeds to "moisten" them and practicing my blowing and deep breathing.

When my family moved farther away from the school, my mom decided to have Mr. Brown come to our house instead. Something inside me snapped. I was never a big fit-pitcher, but I pitched a good one in protest of Mr. Brown tainting our home piano bench with his ass sweat. Some instinct told me that I did not want this man in our house. My mom was as surprised as I was at my extreme reaction. Mr. Brown had never done anything inappropriate to me; he was just a little creepy.

"I just don't like him!" I screamed. "He creeps me out!"

"Okay, okay." My mom relented, probably assuming I was having some sort of dramatic tween breakdown.

So just like that, I was freed from my weekly music lessons and I moved on to after-school swimming lessons in our backyard pool, with a much less creepy teacher.

Shortly after we broke up with Mr. Brown, he disappeared. The tiny school was buzzing with rumors, and it was finally confirmed that Mr. Brown had been caught with underage porn in a sting operation. I was shocked, totally grossed out, and happy I'd never have to moisten a reed in his presence again.

DIY Ironic Art

PREP IT

Artist's canvas, size of your choice

Latex paint, color of your choice

Paint stirrer

Paintbrush

DO IT!

1. Lay the canvas on a surface you don't mind getting painty. Open the can of paint and give it a stir.

2. Paint whatever you want, but don't do it well. No, seriously—the sloppier and quicker, the better. A nice, thick paintbrush and a giant canvas will help give your art some oomph. I chose to paint *I'm not a good painter* and then spill some paint on the edge of the canvas and sign it with a painty thumbprint.

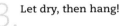
3. Let dry, then hang!

Tip: Another fun idea is painting the entire canvas black and let it dry. Then use white paint to create your letter art.

DO IT Elsewhere! Cut a patch of canvas drop cloth, paint it with something ironic, and safety pin it to your favorite jacket!

Chapter 8

TOM HANKS IS MY BOYFRIEND

When I was little, I could fly. I have distinct memories at around two years old of being able to jump on my bed and then levitate to the ceiling. It wasn't the *zoom* kind of flying; it was more of a slow hover. I remember showing my mom and seeing my stuffed animals from a bird's-eye perspective. I knew not to try to fly outside, because the helpful ceiling stopped my upward float, and outside I might just float up forever. My mom supported my claim, and to this day I still believe I did it.

Years later, at age fourteen, I wore a bathing suit to dinner with Tom Hanks.

We were in London and my dad had a business meeting with Tom at Nobu, a very posh Japanese restaurant. My mom and I met them after their meeting and the four of us ate delicious raw fish together, under the watchful eyes and whispers of the room. Tom was the biggest movie star in the world, and I was wearing a 1940s-style bathing suit at the dinner table. It was an eggplant-colored, crushed velvet, skintight Betsey Johnson creation. The velvet was gloriously soft and reflected the light just so, and in my opinion, it elevated the look from bathing suit to something dinner appropriate. The high neckline balanced out the semiexposed butt cheeks, but let's be honest, it was a bathing suit.

Tom complimented me on my outfit in a very sweet and paternal way. "You look very nice!" he said, sounding friendly and warm and, well, like Tom Hanks. My beaming dad responded, "Kate is always surprising us with her fashion sense, in a good way."

I was always excited to be different. That's what energized me about style—the expression of self. I knew that as I walked through the restaurant, people would form their own opinions about me—"she's a slut," "she's weird," "she's crazy," "she's rebelling," "why are her parents letting her dress like that!?" or maybe "she looks cool"—but it was empowering, because I knew who I was. Strangers would form their own opinions about my perceived lack of parental guidance, but my mom and dad always valued letting me express myself over worrying what everyone else thought.

Later on in the meal, while we were working on our hot sesame oil–seared hamachi, some sycophant in a suit came over to rub palms with Tom and my dad. My dad introduced my mother and I, and the sycophant said, "Oh, this is your daughter? She had all the eyes in the restaurant on her when she walked in. Watch out for this one!" He guffawed and elbowed my dad in that, "Ya get what I'm sayin?" creeper kind of way. It was one of the first times I felt queasy from a man's attention on my choice of clothes; I've always been the type of girl who dresses more for my own amusement than for sexual attention. I always appreciate a compliment more from a gal than a guy. Sure, the choice of wearing a bathing suit in public sounds risqué, but it was more of an art piece than an opportunity to flaunt my junk. My feminist tendencies usually make me choose a diaper-esque, drop-crotch harem pant over a cleavage-baring dress . . . unless the booby-baring number has something gloriously unique about it—pizza print, maybe? But that evening, in a sushi restaurant in London, I was happy with my crushed velvet bathing suit outfit choice, because I liked it and so did Tom Hanks, and we were all that mattered.

I'm eternally grateful that my parents let me partially bare my butt cheeks to Tom Hanks, because—for a fourteen-year-old—that was flying. I levitated on my self-expression but didn't disappear into the clouds, nurturing a self-confidence that later got me through many a debacle. Including when my parents turned into total fucking messes.

#WhyNot **Be different and be you, velvet butt cheeks and all. Float off into your dreams with these Tom Hanks–approved DIY Crushed Velvet Pillows.**

DIY Crushed Velvet Pillows

PREP IT

Yardstick or measuring tape

Throw pillow insert or an old pillow you want to cover

Velvet—enough to cover both sides of the pillow plus a few inches

Fabric scissors

Iron

Hot glue gun and fabric glue sticks

DO IT!

1. Measure and cut two square pieces of velvet 2 inches larger than the pillow on all sides (I cut 22 x 22 inches of fabric for my 20 x 20 inch pillow).

2. Turn on your iron to the silk or poly setting, depending on what type of velvet you have.

3. Gather pleats across the bias of your velvet (diagonally across the grain of the fabric) and iron over the pleats. Let the fabric cool a little, then crumple the pleats in your hand to create a crushed look to accentuate the luxurious fabric. Repeat on both squares until you get your desired crushed look.

4. Lay the two velvet pieces on top of each other with the crushed velvet sides of the fabric facing each other. Peel back the top square and hot glue 1 inch in from the edge on three sides of the square to adhere both faces of the fabric together and create a seam. Tip: Use a yardstick along the fold to give you a straight line to follow with your glue gun.

5. On the fourth side of the square, apply glue a couple of inches in from each corner but leave an unglued area in the center of the fourth side (this is where you'll insert your pillow). Let the glue dry completely.

6. Turn the pillowcase right side out through the opening and carefully stuff the pillow into the opening.

7. Seal the opening by folding the fabric inward to mimic the seam that you already started near the corners, and glue to close. Let dry completely, then style on your bed or couch!

DO IT Elsewhere! Glue fancy velvet ribbon down each leg of an old pair of pants!

Chapter 9
TEENAGE SAINT

Like many children, I was raised with an awareness of magical beings. Those magical beings took the form of the typical fat American Santa, giant white Easter Bunny, and pixie-like Tooth Fairy. My hippie mother also made sure we were visited by the European fringe characters, rarely spotted in the U.S.A.: St. Nicholas, the svelte version of Santa who comes on December 6, and Santa Lucia, the young saint celebrated in Sweden who brings saffron buns and hot chocolate in the wee hours of the morning on December 13. All the magical beings were great because I could just wait around for them to bring me stuff. All except for Santa Lucia . . . because per Scandinavian tradition, I was supposed to act *as* Santa Lucia.

A sister moment by the pool

As the eldest daughter in the family, I had to impersonate the young, blond saint and deliver the fragrant buns and hot chocolate (coffee for the adults) to my three sleeping family members (Mom, Dad, and little sis, Tess). The night before December 13, the smell of sweet saffron spices would waft up from our kitchen and I knew I had an early morning coming. I'd wake to the five A.M. darkness, don my flowing silk robe and the crown of gold chains that my mom DIY'd, pouf out my blond hair Swedish-saint-style, and make the rounds.

In the early years, my dad would quietly wake me for my saintly duties, then go back to bed, but when I got older, I set a saintly alarm . . . don't all saints use alarms? My robe and crown would be laid out on the kitchen island, along with a tray of fresh saffron buns and handwritten instructions on how to brew the coffee and make the hot chocolate. Even though the hour was early, the trays were heavy, and though I was hardly a saint, I felt a duty to my still-believing little sister to pull off the Santa Lucia farce with the precision of RuPaul's dick tuck.

After the hot liquids were brewed, I would load up my tray, light the candle, and gingerly venture up the stairs. I hit up my parents first, creeping into the dark room with my candle flickering and approaching their nightstands. My dad would wake and say, "Hi, Santa Lucia," which is ridiculously cute, now that I think about it, and my mom gave a quiet, "Thank you," as I placed her coffee and bun on the table.

In Tess's room down the hall, I would place her saffron bun and hot chocolate on the bedside table. She would wake up, bleary eyed, and stare at me as I quickly whisked out of the room, white robes flowing. Amazingly, she believed in the magic and would find me later in the morning to tell me excitedly that she saw the back of Santa Lucia and she was "sooo pretty!" It was a spooky and magical tradition until the year Tess decided to chase her favorite blond girl saint.

By this time, Tess was about seven years old and I was thirteen. I dropped off her hot cocoa and bun in my usual saintly fashion, but this year, new internal teen timing in place, I had pushed Santa Lucia's wake-up call a little too late. Rather than just the candlelight illuminating the room, the pesky sun was also starting to rear its bright-ass head. Right after I plopped the saffron bun down on the table, Tess sat up in bed and stared at me.

"Kate?" she said.

Oh, shit, thought Santa Lucia, and I bolted from the room, but Tess started to chase me, bare feet hitting the carpeted hallway after me as I snaked down the stairs and threw myself into the narrow broom closet. Santa Lucia was out of breath, shaking and sweating in her silk robe (the gold crown had been lost somewhere in the ker-fuffle). I heard Tess in front of the broom closet door calling, "Kate? Kate, I saw you!"

I was a covert spy on a mission, and I couldn't blow my cover, so I sat with a dust-pan digging into my robed butt and waited out the little investigating demon. My mom found Tess trying to break into the closet and scooped her away to enjoy her saintly breakfast. I made a stealth exit out of the broom closet, changed back into my pajamas, and sauntered casually into Tess's room. She was sitting on her canopy bed with crumbs on her face, a hot chocolate mustache, and Santa Lucia's tangled crown on her head. "Where were you?" Tess asked skeptically.

I sipped some hot chocolate and said, "What do you mean?"

"I saw Santa Lucia and she looks just like you," Tess said as she looked expectantly at me.

"Really? I look like Santa Lucia?" I said to my messy-haired little sister. "That's awesome. Is she pretty?"

Tess looked relieved and nodded. "Yeah, she has blond hair, but it's longer than yours. Promise it wasn't you?"

It would have been so easy to tell her the truth and get out of waking up so damn early next year, but my heart ached in that moment because I saw a little girl still wanting to believe the world is a magical place.

"Yup," I promised. "I was taking a poop in the bathroom."

The next year, at age eight, my sister was hit by a car in front of our house. I was the only one with her and as she lay bleeding in my arms, she looked up at me and asked, "Am I going to die?" Tapping into my best Santa Lucia, I promised her every-thing would be okay if she believed. In the moment, though, I had no idea if she would live. I called the paramedics and she was okay, apart from a giant scar down her leg. That day, we both learned that the world isn't all saffron buns and hot cocoa, but that magic can still be found in our sisterly bond and Tess can always count on me to lie to her.

‖ #WhyNot **Keep the magic alive and feel like a saint
‖ in a DIY Chain Headpiece.**

DIY Chain Headpiece

PREP IT

Various delicate chains (I chose to mix metal chain with rhinestone chain)

Wire cutters

2 metal hair combs

Jewelry glue, like Dazzle-Tac or E6000

DO IT!

1. Stick the combs in your hair to see how they hold best, then decide how long you want the chains to be for best draping between the combs. I used six chains at varying lengths between 12 and 20 inches. Cut the chains to your desired length with the wire cutters.

2. Use a little dot of glue to adhere the ends of each chain to the base of each comb and connect the combs. Keep in mind the direction you'll be placing the combs in your hair so that the chains drape as desired.

Chapter 10
A HOLE IN ONE

Once upon a time, there was a girl who knew diddly squat about sports (still doesn't) who found herself in bed with the world's most famous athlete.

Hardly an accolade that I go around shouting from the rooftops, but yes, I've had sex with Tiger Woods.

I know, I know, so original . . . join the club, Kate! The truth is this happened years ago, before he was married, so no families were harmed in the making of this story.

I was nineteen and hanging out with my jolly, jet-setting friend Gretchen, who was always going someplace cool with someone famous. One of her very best friends, whom she had a desperate crush on, was a guy named Lee who happens to be Tiger's BFF. The only time I ever saw Gretchen cry was over Lee, so I was led to believe she had very genuine feelings for him. She told me that Lee and Tiger invited her to Atlanta to go to the NBA All-Star Game and said I should totally come. We'd stay at their hotel, they'd comp our room, and "it would be a blast!"

Now, let me state something very important: I know nothing about golf. I didn't then, and I don't now. At that time, I knew Tiger was supposed to be a really good golfer who did a few commercials and won stuff. I had grown up around celebrities and had learned that they're just regular people whose farts smell just like the rest of ours—ahem, Robin Williams, RIP—so I wasn't particularly impressed with the idea of hanging out with professional athletes, but I'd never been to Atlanta, and who am I to pass up an all-expense-paid adventure with one of my besties?! So off I flew to meet Gretchen in the South.

When I got to the hotel, Gretchen was in her usual chill-but-cute Juicy Couture sweatsuit (this was when having the word "juicy" on your ass was at the height of fashion). She was hanging out in Tiger's suite on the couch and jumped up, yelping in delight when I came through the door and giving me a big hug. "Kate, this is Lee and Tiger," she said pointing to the chubby Asian guy on the couch and Tiger, who had gotten up to shake my hand. "I already told them how hilarious you are and that you don't know anything about basketball," Gretchen said, giggling.

"Yes, I can attest to at least the basketball thing. I've got no fucking clue about any sports, but I love hotels!"

I had no idea what to expect from Tiger, because I'd never met a pro golfer before, but he was nice and funny and we all laughed it up until it was time to go to dinner. As Gretchen and I left the room to go get ready, we passed a man in a suit with an earpiece stationed outside the hotel room next to Tiger's.

"Is that his bodyguard?" I asked Gretchen. "He looks very serious."

Gretchen whispered, "No, that's Secret Service. Bill Clinton is staying in the suite next door to Tiger."

"Ohhhh, cool!" I said. I was way more impressed with an ex-president than any golfer or basketball player. Heck, I was super impressed with the Secret Service agent himself—he looked so lethal!

Gretchen and I got dressed for dinner, which would be in the hotel restaurant. The thing I was learning about Tiger was that he was pretty low maintenance and didn't really like to venture out unless he had to. That was fine with me, even though I was curious to explore the city; I was hungry, and since I was under twenty-one, a hotel restaurant sounded like a good bet for getting an alcoholic drink.

I wore my cutest pair of flared-leg jeans with rainbow Miu Miu platforms in a feeble attempt to decrease the height difference between the pro athletes and my pro short-girl stature. As we left our room to head to the elevator, I was still buckling the ankle strap on my platforms when I heard Gretchen giggle and say, "Hi, Mr. President!" I looked up and nearly crotch-butted one of the Secret Service agents flanking Bill Clinton on his way into his suite. "Oh! Hi, Mr. President!" I giddily repeated, like I was running into Justin Timberlake–era *NSYNC.

In the elevator, Gretchen turned to me and said conspiratorially, "I think Tiger likes you."

I was skeptical. "Why?"

"He doesn't usually laugh that much. He seems like he's having a really good time, and he's usually mega serious," she said knowingly. "Lee and I kept glancing at each other. I think he can tell, too."

"Huh," I said, flattered. "Well, I guess he's cute and nice, and he knows how to swing his stick."

Gretchen guffawed, and we headed to Tiger's table in the back corner of the restaurant. Tiger and Lee were sitting in the booth with some other sporty-looking guys, who turned out to be Michael Jordan, Charles Barkley, and some ESPN guy. I was pretty aware of Michael Jordan from sneakers, if nothing else.

As I'd hoped, they don't card you when you're sitting in a hotel restaurant with Tiger and Michael, so Gretchen and I proceeded to get drunk on cosmos—yes, it was the height of the cosmopolitan's reign on mixed drinks.

"All of your fascination with balls is concerning!" I said, in an attempt to join the sports-focused conversation at the table. "Let's talk about how you've all decorated your mansions. Michael, you first!" Most at the table laughed, especially Tiger.

Tiger was sitting next to me in the horseshoe-shaped booth, and I could feel some chemistry heating up between us. He turned to me and asked if I was having fun.

"Totally," I said. "This is a very unique experience. Thank you to you and the Democratic Party for having me."

He laughed.

"I like your hair," Tiger said. I wore my curly blond mop in a wild bob at the time.

"Thanks! It's a little crazy," I said, grinning. "Like me!" Ugh, these cosmos were making me frisky. Charles Barkley leaned over on my opposite side and said, with a twinkle in his eye, something about my hair not being "nappy" and how I had some *reeeal* nice curls.

"Gotcha," I said. "Can I get another cosmo?" I was focused on taking this night to the next level with Tiger, not having an in-depth conversation about hair texture with Charles Barkley, although it was actually a topic I knew something about.

Tiger kept turning to me and smiling shyly. It was cute. I liked his understated flirtation, and knowing Gretchen would probably be hooking up with her love, Lee, I figured I'd let this fun chemistry take over. An hour or so into dinner, I felt Tiger's foot hit mine under the table. At first I thought it was an accident, and then I realized he was playing footsie with me! I playfully kicked him back and we grinned at each other. *Is this really happening? He's such a cute dork!* I thought. The fact that his tactic was footsie was totally endearing.

Lee, Gretchen, Tiger, and I made our way back to Tiger's room to hang out some more. I was coming to realize that famous athletes love hotel rooms and hotel bars and are apparently allergic to the outside world. I waved to the Secret Service agent stationed between Tiger's and Bill Clinton's suite doors.

"The boss in for the night?" I asked the agent. "Ha, I know you can't tell me that! Nice suit, you look really pulled together this evening."

After stumbling into the hotel room, we convinced the boys to have a somersault contest since it had been so long since I'd done one and I wanted to see how mine compared to a pro athlete's. Tired and happy, Gretchen and Lee then retired to our room, leaving Tiger and me sitting on his couch. He leaned over and kissed me, a nice, soft kiss. He was shy, so that was my cue to jump on his lap, growl, and start making out more ferociously. He laughed and said, "You're wild!"

"Shut up," I said. "I'm refereeing this game!"

Do they have referees in golf?

We had a fun sexual romp, and I remember wondering if Bill Clinton could hear us through the shared wall. Tiger fell asleep, but I was too wired and wanted to tell Gretchen what happened, so I snuck out. Waving at the Secret Service agent, I thought to myself, *It's probably a once-in-a-lifetime experience for your walk of shame to be supervised by the Secret Service.* I awkwardly gave the agent a salute and said, "Hole in one!"

#WhyNot **If you're not good at sports, you can still have fun with balls. Make these DIY Ping-Pong Marquee Letters to score some bright style points in your interior space.**

DIY Ping-Pong
Marquee Letters

PREP IT

Craft knife

Papier-mâché letters (see
Resources, page 272)

Drop cloth

Spray paint, color of your choice

LED twinkle lights (4 to 5 boxes,
depending on your word length)

White Ping-Pong balls
(10 to 12 for each letter)

Twine

Picture ledge shelf, long enough
for your word

Level

Screws and anchors for securely
mounting the shelf

DO IT!

1. Use the craft knife to cut out the backs
of your letters.

2. Set up the drop cloth outside and
spray paint the letters the color of your
choice. Let dry for about 1 hour. You may
want to apply two coats.

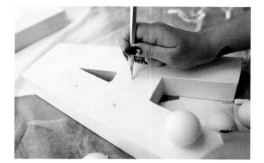

5. Starting with the first letter in your word, grab a string of twinkle lights and push the lightbulbs through the "X" cuts from the back. Connect another string of lights as needed, going from letter to letter and storing the cord and any extra bulbs in the hollow back of a letter if you need to.

3. On the front side of each letter, make evenly spaced "X" cuts along the center of the shape of the letter, where you want the lights to show. I left 2½ to 3 inches between each cut.

6. Make a small "X" cut on one Ping-Pong ball for each lightbulb that's showing. Push a ball onto each lightbulb.

7. Wrap any cord that shows with twine for a more finished look. Tip: Tie a knot every 10 to 15 wraps to keep the twine from unraveling.

8. Hang the picture ledge using a level and the appropriate nails or screws for your wall.

4. Think about where you plan to display the word and make sure the plug end of a string of twinkle lights will be where you need it.

9. Arrange the marquee letters, tucking the connecting cord behind the lip of the picture ledge, and plug in your new light art!

Chapter 11
MAKE-BELIEVE BULLIES

"Cut!" yelled the director. "This time smear the jizz into her face a little more!"

The actress looked at me and mouthed "sorry" as the makeup artist wiped the jizz from the previous take off my lips and I spit into a napkin she held up.

"Action!"

The actress's face contorted into her mean girl sorority character and she glopped a handful of fake male ejaculate on my mouth and rubbed it in.

I was twenty-two and had been cast in one of the lead roles playing a well-intentioned but extremely awkward sorority pledge in an independent film (you could probably rent it if you wanted to, but I advise having a drink or a good book nearby). The dark comedy starred Haylie Duff as the pretty, pulled-together sorority president. Haylie's character and the entire sorority sets out to dissuade me at all costs from joining their ranks, even though my character is a legacy, which is supposed to give me an automatic in.

I was excited to be a lead and to be playing what I'd imagined to be a fun and challenging character. In preparation for the role, my hair was stripped of all my usual blond highlights—an investment down the drain. They fitted me for a fake pink retainer, fulfilling a childhood dream. And to plump up, my diet consisted of scones and milkshakes— fulfilling all my adult dreams.

In addition to getting fake jizz (a combo of petroleum jelly and white eye shadow) smeared on my face, the script called for all kinds of mortifying scenarios filmed in front of a giant cast, crew, and hundreds of extras.

Like Jackie Chan, I do most of my own stunts.

The night of the Jell-O wrestling scene, it was 40 degrees out and I was already freezing in my character's tank top and maxi skirt. By this point in the script, the sorority girls had gotten my character sloppy drunk and challenged me to get in the giant rubber pool filled with Jell-O to wrestle with two bikini-clad stuntgirls. Oblivious to their evil plot, I enthusiastically belly flop in, fully clothed, to the cheers of the yard full of college kid extras.

The minuscule independent movie budget meant that everything about the production was janky. Whatever genius they had in charge of getting the Jell-O wrestling pool together had started it too late in the day, and by nightfall the Jell-O hadn't firmed up. It was a giant bowl of red fucking liquid. They scrambled to help it solidify by pointing giant ducts of air from the studio directly at the kiddie pool. That didn't work, so they resorted to spooning premade Jell-O from those tiny snack cups into the giant rubber pool so that "at least" there were some solid chunks floating around in the red liquid nightmare.

Stained red, with my teeth chattering inside my retainer, I faced the buff bikini duo as they swung me around, take after take, letting me face-plant in the frigid Jell-NO.

For the grand finale, these bikini-clad cunts pulled down my soaking wet maxi skirt to reveal my giant "granny" panties for the whole party to see. The women attacked my lower half and I tried desperately to hold on to the front of the skirt so at least the extras couldn't see my vagina—the red water had made the underwear more sheer than I had anticipated. Make believe or not, my basic survival instincts took over at times—it was hard to remember that I was getting paid to do this. My feeble attempts to fight back just found me sliding down the length of a slimy buff girl, clutching at boobs and kneecaps, only to find myself submerged and seriously considering a career change.

"Cut!" yelled the director for the millionth time. "Kate, can you scream louder after they pants you?"

#WhyNot **Stick it to them and make the most out of a prickly situation. Do your own stunts and bejewel a DIY Pretty and Prickly Cactus.**

DIY Pretty and Prickly Cactus

PREP IT

Drop cloth

Foam paintbrush

Potted cactus

White acrylic paint

Pastel acrylic paint(s) in color(s) of your choice

Earrings, pins, and brooches

DO IT!

1. **Cover a work surface with the drop cloth. Using a foam paintbrush, paint the cactus pot with the white paint and let it dry.**

2. Paint over the white with the pastel color(s). (The white paint keeps you from having to do too many coats of pastel.)

3. Push the pins of your jewelry pieces into the body of the cactus, taking care not to get pricked!

DO IT Elsewhere! Use clip-on earrings as shoe clips for a quick and shiny shoe bedazzle.

Chapter 12

POMEGRANATES AND PORN

I lost my innocence in the pomegranate field next to my childhood school.

I was in the fourth grade, and my friend Missy and I would sneak over the fence after school to pick the forbidden fruit from the rows and rows of trees. Apparently pomegranates make everyone feel intoxicated with passions of the flesh, because there were often empty beer bottles and scraps of nudie magazines left under the fruiting trees—probably left there by the workers constructing a nearby church.

Missy and I would fill our sweatshirt pockets with the round, red fruits and try not to drop them in a bloody splat on the climb back over the school fence. My mom would pick us up and drive us home and never seemed miffed that we were carrying armfuls of juicy contraband. It was good, clean fun!

One day while Missy and I were trying to decide which tree had the reddest fruit, we came across a book of porn. It wasn't a torn and dirt-smeared piece of magazine; this was a paperback book with black-and-white photos of people having sex. "Ugh, look, this lady has one guy behind her and one by her face!" exclaimed Missy. I couldn't believe my fourth-grade eyes, "That's possible?" I wondered aloud, feeling that tingle in my groin that I felt when I humped my stuffed animals. Holy pomegranates, this was a great find!

We nervously chattered in hushed tones, even though we were alone in the field, as each salacious image tainted our brains. Our most important question was: How do we take this book with us? It was too good to leave behind for the beer-drinking wolves. My mom was used to us getting in the car with pomegranates, but not porn. Missy wanted to hide it under a tree for us to pore over the next day, but I needed to look at it again that night. I knew this was going to be the best hump session of my life—that stuffed bear didn't know what he was in for.

Missy begged me to leave the book so we wouldn't get in trouble, and there was no way she was going to keep it at her house and risk a porn encounter of the scary kind with her formidable mother. But my mind, clouded by passion in the pomegranate field, decided I could hide the book up the sleeve of my jacket.

Missy and I casually sauntered to my mom's car, with our usual hoard of pomegranates. The book was threatening to slip out of my sleeve, but I kept my arm bent, holding on to my fruit. In the backseat of the car (I wasn't allowed to sit in the front, still too short), Missy was nervously darting glances at me, and I shot her a look that said, *Eyes on the road, partner.*

We dropped Missy off at her house and pulled into our driveway. I jumped out, pretending to be really excited to go eat my pomegranates in my room. Once behind closed doors, I tore through some more photos and then ransacked my stuffed animal pile looking for the *perrrfect* hump.

I hid the book on the side of my bed where it met the wall. Everyone hides stuff under their bed, but the side seemed like a safer choice. A couple of days went by in a cloud of raunchy bliss—pomegranates and porn, pomegranates and porn—until one fateful afternoon when my mom said, "I need to talk to you about something."

My heart plummeted to my horny toes.

"What?" I asked.

"I was putting that new quilt I made you on your bed today and I found a very inappropriate book."

Nooo, I thought. *She's going to make me get rid of it!* I was humiliated. I couldn't let her think it was mine.

"Missy found it and gave it to me to keep so her mom wouldn't get mad at her," I lied. "It's not mine."

"I don't care whose it is," my mom replied, calmly but sternly. "There are some things that are not appropriate for someone your age to see. When we get home today, I want you to go straight into your room, get the book, and throw it out in the trash can on the street."

She knew if it was in the house, I'd fish it out of the trash and find a better hiding spot.

"Okay," I muttered, not at all pleased that I had to throw away such a close friend.

"I won't watch you," my mom said, "but when you've thrown it away, come and tell me it's done. I'm trusting you to do this."

I nodded.

I slowly entered my room and found the book, still stashed next to my bed. I took one last, good, hard, long look at some of my favorite images of those ladies with eighties hair and those men with mustaches doing things I wouldn't do myself for many years, if ever. I glumly walked outside the house to the trash cans. I wonder if anyone on our cul-de-sac that day noticed the nine-year-old sadly throwing away a perfectly good paperback book of porn. I said my good-byes as I stuffed it deep down in that trash can, leaving it as a piece of trash, the same way I had found it in the pomegranate field four days prior. One man's trash is another woman's pleasure.

Inside the house, I found my mom in the kitchen, poked my head in the doorway, and said, "It's done."

She nodded, and I retreated to my room to mourn the loss of the loss of my innocence.

#WhyNot **Inspired by juicy pomegranates, bring pleasure to your interior space with a sexy DIY Pom-Pom Chair.**

DIY Pom-Pom Chair

PREP IT

Chair with a removable cushion

100-grit sandpaper

Drop cloth

Spray paint, in the color(s) of your choice

Hot glue gun and glue sticks

Yarn pom-poms, in the colors and sizes of your choice (my chair took 120 pom-poms); make them yourself (see next page) or check the Resources (page 272)

DO IT!

1. Remove the cushion from your chair. Tip: If there are screws holding the cushion in place, you can usually use a screwdriver to loosen the screws underneath the cushion.

2. Use the sandpaper to sand off any peeling paint or smooth any rough patches on the chair.

3. Spread out a drop cloth outside and spray paint the chair. Tip: You might want to use a spray paint primer first if you're painting a light color over a dark chair, to make it pop. Let the paint dry, then do more coats as needed to get the color you want.

4. Hot-glue the pom-poms to the cushion, taking care to bunch them close together so that the cushion fabric doesn't show underneath.

5. Reattach the cushion and take a seat! You deserve a nice rest.

DO IT Elsewhere! Make your own pom-poms using a fork, yarn, and scissors. Wrap yarn 15 to 20 times around the fork and knot a separate piece of yarn tightly around the middle to cinch the bundle. Cut through each outer edge of the wrapped yarn to release it from the fork, then plump your handmade pom-pom!

Chapter 13

A TRIBE CALLED TAMPON

In my sophomore year of high school we had a unit on Native American culture. This was a special three-week block taught by our usual history teacher, Mr. Baker, and a guest teacher, Mr. Daniels, a Native American culture enthusiast. We spent two weeks studying different tribes and their histories, and on the third week we took a class camping trip to a Native American reservation near New Mexico. We would hike ten miles into the reservation and spend four nights sleeping under the stars, exploring the ancient cliff dwellings and re-creating some Native American rituals.

Mr. Baker and Mr. Daniels gave us a packing list, which included warm sleeping bags, something to wear while in a sweat lodge, and for the girls, plastic bags in which to keep your used sanitary napkins and tampons. According to Mr. Daniels, these were not to be left in the sacred canyon, per the supposed Native American cultural rules.

"What if they're biodegradable?" I had asked, raising my hand and getting some grossed-out stares from my male classmates. Mr. Daniels gravely shook his gray-haired head. "It's not about littering," he said. "You don't want to insult the ancient spirits by leaving your menstrual blood behind in the sacred canyon." He went on to tell us that menstruating women were traditionally required to be isolated in a hut and not participate in any rituals or ceremonies. Mr. Daniels said that if we were on our period while on the trip, we had to be honest and not participate in the sweat lodge. Mr. Daniels was a creep.

On week three, our class of twenty-three kids, plus the two teachers and some chaperones, packed our backpacks and headed to New Mexico, where I promptly started my period.

My period was irregular in my teenage years, so I never knew when I'd start making prune juice, but I had packed some tampons just in case. I started surfing the crimson wave on the drive to the sacred canyon. The first night we spent outside the reservation, so I indulged myself by throwing my used tampons in the trash can. The next day, led by our Native American guide, we walked the long, hot hike onto the sacred land. If someone had to pee, we'd stop to find a bush. I was mortified that I had to change my tampon and keep it in a bag. *What if the bag fell out of my backpack?* I wondered, horrified at the thought of the clear plastic baggie with bloody tampons falling onto the dirt trail in front of my fifteen-year-old classmates, grossing them all out and causing me the most embarrassing moment ever. *That would suck!* I shuddered at the thought and kept hiking the dusty trail into the gorgeous box canyon.

I didn't know how to feel about this whole period punishment. My mom had raised me to celebrate my menstrual cycle, and my burgeoning inner feminist was rather incensed at the thought that my natural bodily functions might insult the spirits in the canyon.

We got to the campsite and would spend the next three days and nights investigating the ancient cliff dwellings and sleeping under the stars. My plastic bag of used tampons with their strings hanging was starting to resemble a tangled mound of dead, bloody mice. It was such a hassle to covertly stuff the bag in my sweatshirt pocket, walk to the secluded bucket that was our toilet, change my tampon, and then cram the bag back in my backpack without anyone witnessing the transfer. The spirits were really getting on my nerves.

On the second day, I reached my breaking point. There were too many boys around to keep transferring the plastic bag in broad daylight, so on my next trip to the bucket to change my tampon, I took a detour to a large bush. I removed my tampon and buried it in a little hole I dug under the bush. I said aloud to the sacred canyon, "Sorry, spirits of the ancestors, but my tampons are one hundred percent biodegradable organic cotton, and my period is not gross."

Later that evening, our guide prepared us for a vision quest ceremony, a deeply spiritual experience in which you spend time with nature in complete solitude for up to four days and nights. Thankfully, they condensed our vision quest into a three-hour retreat, but it was still after the sun had set, when the sacred valley was lit only by the moon.

I was, and still am, afraid of the dark. I was petrified as the guide led me away from the group to a secluded area, shrouded by bushes. He instructed me to sit on the hard ground until I heard the call to come back to camp.

"What if I get eaten by a wolf?" I asked him.

He laughed. "There are no wolves here, just coyotes, and they don't want to eat you."

"They might!" I said. "I'm small and tasty." Remembering that you're not supposed to go swimming with sharks when you're on your period, I was especially afraid that I smelled like menstrual blood. But I couldn't bring myself to tell the guide about my period—I didn't want any more shame! So I sat, scared shitless, looking up at the mass of glittering stars and knowing that my death was near. I had left my tampon buried in the sacred dirt, and now the spirits had the perfect opportunity to smite me for my sins.

What happened over the next couple of hours was, in fact, a spiritual experience, because I survived. The spirits didn't send a pack of coyotes to eat me alive—they let me enjoy the glory of the canyon. I slowly relaxed and took in the immense cliffs around me, the moonlight coloring them a beautiful baby blue with the sounds of insects chirping in symphony. I knew this was a sign. I had survived because Mr. Daniels was wrong—the gods loved a good period!

I heard the caw of the guide to return back to camp, and I triumphantly skipped my way back to the group. I was alive and bleeding.

#WhyNot **Connect with your animal spirit by making a DIY Cruelty-Free Feather Crown for all your style quests.**

DIY Cruelty-Free
Feather Crown

PREP IT

1½- to 2-inch-wide
ribbon

Cruelty-free feathers
(see Resources, page 272)

Hot glue gun and glue
sticks

Decorative lace trim a bit
wider than your ribbon

DO IT!

1. Cut two pieces of ribbon: one to fit
around your head with enough length
to tie in back and the other to fit across the
front of your forehead from ear to ear.

2. Plan your feather layout on the smaller
piece of ribbon and hot-glue the
feathers in place.

3. Center the longer piece of ribbon to cover the bottom of the feathers on the shorter piece of ribbon and glue it in place.

4. Glue a piece of lace trim over the ribbon base at the front of your crown.

5. Tie your crown around your head and style with whatever outfit makes you feel like a queen!

DO IT Elsewhere! Remove the paper from an old lampshade to expose the wire frame and use thin wire or fishing line to tie feathers on for a bohemian-chic look!

Chapter 14
A BUNK BUILT FOR TWO

Joey and I had been "dating" long distance for a month when he invited me to join him on tour for a few nights. I'd never been on a tour bus before, and I was so excited to see Joey and experience the rock star life.

I showed up in my Louboutin pumps with my rolling luggage, ready for a glamorous experience. Joey laughed at the size of my suitcase and led me down the narrow hallway to the back of the tour bus, where he plunked it down on the horseshoe-shaped bench in the postage-stamp-size "lounge."

"Try to keep it neat so the other dudes don't get annoyed," Joey said with a smirk. "I'm already breaking the rules by having you stay with us for more than one night."

Uh oh, I thought. *How am I supposed to blow-dry my hair? I don't want four skinny, angry musicians glaring at me while I'm trying to pick out my cute groupie outfits!* This lounge was the only area that actually had a door, but it was still, like the rest of the bus, community territory.

"I'll show you my bed," Joey said, brushing his shaggy hair out of his eyes. I had to stop myself every second from latching onto his face and smothering him with kisses. He was so darn sexy.

Me and Joey on the tour bus couch on the way to a new city

His "bed" was more like a cot—a cubby, if you will—that was five feet off the ground and over someone else's "bed." That someone was Ethan, the bass player. I had to step on Ethan's bed to hoist my short body up into Joey's bed, which I found to be narrower than a twin bed!

"We're both sleeping in here?" I asked.

"Yup," Joey said, laughing in his signature adorable, contagious, high-pitched giggle, "Don't worry, it can work—I've done it before."

Eww. I'd rather not imagine what other female bodies had been crammed in there with my man candy, but hey, that comes with the territory when you're dating a pop star with adoring fans currently standing outside of the bus . . . at the blow-job ready.

We'd drive mostly at night, after the boys were done with their concerts. Joey would shower off his drummer sweat in the two-foot-square shower, holding on to the railing so he didn't fall naked into the hallway as the bus swayed down the highway. Then we'd have some beers with the other guys in the front "lounge," and finally retire to the shelf that was Joey's bed and have the world's bumpiest sex.

Things to keep in mind while having sex in a tour bus bunk:

- Danger: low ceilings! Don't hit your head while on top. The flip-down DVD player/TV combo really leaves an impression.
- Hold on and don't fall out of the cubby; the floor is five feet below.
- Don't be too loud, because there is someone else two feet away, on all sides.
- Don't be alarmed when you hear one of those other people having sex as well.
- Going around wide turns makes the curtain covering the bunk flare out, exposing any bare ass cheeks.
- Don't step on the bass player's face on your way down from the bunk to go for your after-sex pee.

In addition to the five band members and me, there was one tour manager, one guitar tech, one intern, and one loud-mouthed bus driver, all eating, sleeping, and showering on the bus. I quickly learned the most important, unbreakable rule: *Don't poop on the bus.*

Yes, there was a bathroom, but it was only for pee-pee. Poo-poo would fester in the tank, clog up the tiny toilet, and make everyone miserable. If you had to poop, you had to let everyone know, so they could stop the bus at the nearest rest stop or gas station. Needless to say, I didn't go number two much that week—I wasn't going to tell my dream guy when I had to poop. I had to keep some mystery in our brand-new relationship! I would covertly do my doo-doo at radio stations when they were being interviewed or at the concert venues during sound check, but I was way off my usual schedule.

For whatever annoying reason, girls are usually more reserved about sharing their poop habits. The band boys, on the other hand, had no shame in announcing when they had to poo, and the only time that Joey had me questioning my complete obsession with him was when he pooped in a bag.

Joey always liked to torture Ben, the keyboard player, who is a germaphobe and really easy to tease. Maybe it was one too many beers or a weird animal mating display, but after one of their shows, Joey decided it would be hilarious to poop in a plastic bag and chase Ben through the tour bus with it in hand. Ben was horrified and so was I, but you know it's true love when you can see someone's turd in a bag and still want to have sex with them later in a tiny cubby.

#WhyNot **When the tour bus is a rockin', don't lose those fabulous heels! These beautiful DIY Bow Heels are made to stay on.**

DIY Bow Heels

PREP IT

Wide wired ribbon that matches the shoes

Sturdy scissors

A pair of appropriate shoes

Thin ribbon that matches the shoes

Hot glue gun and glue sticks

DO IT!

1. Cut two pieces of wide wired ribbon to fit around your ankle, with ample slack to tie a nice big bow (I used about 1 yard for each shoe). Make angled cuts at the end of the ribbons to prevent fraying.

2. Cut two small (about 4-inch) pieces of the thin ribbon and fold them in half to create loop tabs. Depending on the width of your ankle ribbon, the loop should extend about 1 inch above the back of the shoe (smaller than the width of your ankle ribbon, to keep it secure). Glue the tabs to the inside of the back of each shoe, about ½ to 1 inch down, and let the glue dry completely. Pull the thick ribbon through the loop tab on each shoe—it should gather so it fits snugly through the tab.

3. Wear the shoes with the ankle ribbon tied in a big bow in the front or wrapped around once with a smaller bow tied in back.

DO IT Elsewhere! Hot-glue a wide-ribbon bow with a contrasting center tab to a barrette for a *bow-utiful* hair accessory!

Chapter 15

OPEN CASKET CRAZY

My grandmother died. She was my mom's mom and had seven crazy children. Joey, my mom, my sister, Tess, and I flew to Maine for the funeral. My mom and her siblings have never gotten along, so we hadn't been in the same room with our sixteen cousins since probably never. We all uttered awkward hellos to one another in our grandparents' tiny kitchen, where we'd all spent numerous childhood hours during our solo visits but never as a giant family.

Grandpa was very sad to lose Grandma. He was from a lower-class family of French descent and she was a buxom New Englander whom he wooed upon his return from World War II, having fought valiantly as a marine, with post-traumatic stress and agoraphobia as his medals from the war. The funeral was to be held in their hometown of Lewiston, Maine—a real armpit that my mom had run away from during her senior year of high school.

Grandpa is warm and fun and has an amazing sense of humor, cracking nonstop jokes while he cooks a mean tomato sauce, even though he doesn't have an Italian bone in his body. To see Grandpa so sad made me want to help ensure that the funeral went as well as possible.

Then the Irish landed.

My aunt Ella has terrible taste in men. Her first husband cheated on her with dudes, her next boyfriend was a freeloader who left owing my mom twenty thousand dollars, another winning schmuck nearly punched Joey in the face, and then there was her latest catch, the Irishman. Ella had just begun dating this Irish guy, and in the throes of new love, she invited him to her mother's funeral.

As easygoing as Grandpa is, he never liked Ella's taste in boyfriends, who would move in with her and her three kids at record speed. The Irishman's presence during this difficult time was clearly wearing on Grandpa. Whenever the Irishman was near, Grandpa would quietly glare and become uncharacteristically unfriendly.

The whole family busied ourselves with funeral preparations. I was in charge of displaying my grandma's artwork; she had been an incredible artist her whole life, so it was easy to beautify the funeral room with her colorful paintings. My mom assigned herself the role of corpse makeup artist and applied a thick coat of red lipstick to my grandma's reposing lips.

On the day of the funeral, we all sat down at the open-casket ceremony, attended only by family, close friends, and the Irish boyfriend. One of my uncles led the service, standing at the podium positioned next to the open coffin holding my grandma. A couple of my mother's siblings spoke in turn, and I got up as well to tell a story about Grandma teaching me how to paint palm trees on one of her visits to LA.

The funeral was moving along normally until I realized the Irishman was standing in the back with a piece of paper in his hand. My aunt Ella turned around in her seat and asked, very audibly so the whole room could hear, if he was ready to go up to the podium.

He shook his head and said back, loudly, "No, I want to go last," in his thick Irish brogue.

If Grandma thought she was going to get all the attention by lying there in the open casket with her red lipstick on, she was dead wrong. The whole room tensed up, realizing that this random dude was planning some kind of grand finale.

My stomach was in knots. This blowhard had met my family three days earlier, he hadn't even known my grandma, and he was positioning himself to give the closing speech!? If Grandpa didn't hate him enough already, this was going to seal his fate. The suspense was killing me.

After the final sniffling preteen cousin had made her adorably sad speech, my clueless, love-struck aunt proudly ushered her new boyfriend to the podium. Grandiosely plopping down his tiny piece of Ramada Inn stationery, he dramatically cleared his throat. I looked fearfully at Grandpa. His tear-stained face was red—no longer a sad red but a furious scarlet as he silently glared at the man at the podium next to his dead wife. Mom looked back at me and widened her eyes as if to say, *Is this shit fucking happening right now!?* I shrunk down in my chair, digging my decked-out nail art talons into Joey's arm.

The Irishman began, in his thick accent:

These last two days, I bore witness to a family.
I bore witness to a man
I bore witness to a woman
I bore witness to a town,

What is this, fucking Keats? Is he reciting poetry? What. Is. This?

I bore witness to children,
I bore witness to tears
I bore witness to caring
I bore witness to strength
I bore witness to clam chowder
I bore witness . . .

Suddenly, like a B-29 bomber, Grandpa swooped in with a cacophonous coughing fit. He buckled down in his seat, hacking and woofing. Everyone looked concerned and at the same time dumbfounded by the train wreck that was unfolding.

My uncle put his arm around Grandpa, patting him on the back, but to no avail. The Irishman tried to increase his volume as he continued "boring witness" while Grandpa kept coughing. It was an epic battle of lung power between an aging Frenchman and an egomaniacal Irishman.

Coughing and reciting. Hacking and ranting.

My aunt Ella looked annoyed that her beau's speech was being interrupted by my grandpa's rattle. For a moment I actually thought that Grandpa might die, too—his cough was really convincing. But then it hit me: My valiant war veteran grandfather was distracting the enemy. Grandpa was weakening the Irishman's horrible poetic onslaught in as polite a way as possible at his wife's funeral.

The Irishman gave up and retreated to his plastic chair next to Aunt Ella, and the tiny Frenchman quit his coughing. Grandpa had won the battle. I retracted my talons from Joey's welted forearm and silently told Grandma, *You're lucky you weren't here for this.*

#WhyNot **Make the most out of a grating experience with this colorful DIY Sandpaper Art.**

DIY Sandpaper Art

PREP IT

3 or 4 sheets of coarse-grit sandpaper

Acrylic paint, in the color(s) of your choice

Plate or painter's palette

Medium-size artist's paintbrush

Ruler

Thin black marker

Craft knife

Cutting board

Picture frame of your desired size

Thick paper that fits your frame

Hot glue gun and glue sticks

DO IT!

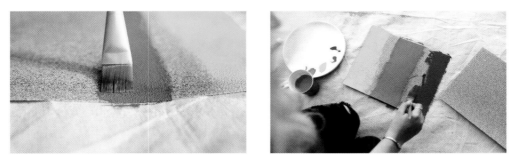

1. Paint stripes using the paint color(s) of your choice on the sandpaper sheets—
I left some parts unpainted as well to show the natural color of the sandpaper. Let dry.

2. Use the ruler and marker to draw a triangle shape on the back of the sandpaper sheet. Cut out the triangle using the craft knife on a cutting board. Tip: Use the first triangle as the template to trace triangles all over the back of the sandpaper sheet.

3. On a thick sheet of paper, lay out the triangles in your desired design and color scheme, using a ruler to help ensure straight lines across the paper backing. Lay the frame on top to make sure the design fits to your liking, then hot-glue the triangles in place. Let dry completely.

4. Frame and hang your art!

DO IT Elsewhere! Make a cute cat greeting card with a painted sandpaper tongue!

Chapter 16
PB&J ON A YACHT

When I was fifteen, I visited my friend Ava on her yacht in the Mediterranean. Well, it was her family's yacht—her dad is a big show biz dude, and they have a jet and a yacht that roams the globe all year. They fly to meet the 172-foot beauty in the Caribbean in the winter and in the Mediterranean in the summer. I knew Ava from horseback riding; competing in the English Hunter/Jumper horse shows introduced me to a whole new level of LA wealth that my San Fernando Valley hippie school knew not of.

That summer, I flew with my dad to meet the boat in Naples. He dropped me off and continued to London for business. I was so excited because I'd never slept on a boat before and was looking forward to my extended sleepover with Ava.

I figured it would be nice, and classy, to bring her family a thank-you gift for having me on the boat for a week and flying me home on their plane. But what do you get the super rich? I wasn't really used to buying extravagant gifts. Even though my dad's job had taken off and we had ascended into the world of the well-off, our ranch house in the Valley was still nothing compared to Ava's Brentwood compound, a stone's throw from OJ Simpson's mansion. I had more tempered taste and always shopped for my crazy clothes at the mall and funky Melrose Avenue thrift stores, but Ava and her family had the taste for luxury and I knew Contempo Casuals would not suffice for my gift-buying needs. So I headed to Rodeo Drive.

Manuel, our gardener-slash-driver, drove me the forty-five minutes from the Valley to Beverly Hills. He was a jolly man from El Salvador whose duties ranged from grooming my mom's extensive rose garden to mucking out horse stalls to driving my sister and me the forty-minute commute to and from school. Manuel supervised my driver's training when I got my permit—the first thing my parents gave up with our newfound wealth was hands-on parenting. Although Manuel was supposed to double as our family's "professional driver," the car my parents gave him to haul us around was a red Dodge Durango SUV, hardly the blacked-out Mercedes of his chauffeur contemporaries.

That summer's day, Manuel dropped me off in the red Durango on Rodeo Drive so I could shop for a yacht-warming gift. I didn't know which store to go to, but I figured Rodeo was the poshest of the posh, and I was bound to find something multimillionaire appropriate that I could hopefully afford with my saved birthday money. I went into Louis Vuitton and contemplated buying a suitcase, but then I figured that would be a bitch to fly with unless I was going to pack stuff in it. Christian Dior and Chanel sold only clothing, and I really wanted to get something the whole family could enjoy. I continued on my trek down Rodeo, with Manuel tailing me in the Durango. I finally found myself inside the Versace store, which had a large display of gold-embroidered beach towels. I thought, *This is perfect! A boat is on water, so you must get wet at some point. Some fancy-schmancy towels might be exactly what a wet millionaire needs!*

I checked the price. *$250 for a towel!?* I inwardly exclaimed, not wanting the already cynical salespeople to get a whiff of my teenage sticker shock. I was having my own *Pretty Woman* moment. I'm sure the salespeople were thinking, *Who is this girl with a blond Afro and vinyl pants inspecting our beach towels? Must be Eurotrash.*

I was excited to show them who was boss. "I'll take five of those sparkly guys," I said, pointing to the black-and-gold filigree towels, a late 1990s design moment at its finest, I'm sure.

Hauling two giant bags full of beach towels, at a price that could feed a large family for a year (somewhere not near Rodeo), I climbed back into the Durango and said to Manuel, "Back to the Valley, kind sir!" I was ready for my glamorous vacation.

The first day on the boat, I grandiosely presented the family with the most expensive towels money can buy. They opened the swanky packaging and graciously thanked me for the colorful monstrosities. My meticulously selected millionaire thank-you towels were added to a giant pile of equally insanely priced designer towels, and we were on our way.

The trip was gorgeous. We meandered around the gleaming Mediterranean Sea, stopping each day at different ports to enjoy the towns of Saint-Tropez, Venice, Santorini, Monte Carlo, Ibiza, and on and on. If Ava and I were too tired from the prior night of partying at the European dance clubs—they totally don't card you in Europe—we would sun ourselves all day on the giant padded beds on the upper deck with one of the twelve crew members bringing us drinks. If at any point you got bored on the giant boat, there were baby boats stored in its loins that you could take out around the magnificent rocky cliffs or to a deserted beach nearby.

Everything was so luxurious, except for the attitudes of the millionaire children. Ava got along horribly with her two brothers. She was the middle child, and the way they all fought with one another was traumatizing. They were in paradise but fought as if they were scrambling for food in a bombed-out village. Ava's older brother picked on her about her weight, and she teased him about his tic. The truth was, he did have the oddest tic—he would squeak like a mouse under his breath. At first I thought it was a normal boat sound—*Oh, I guess yacht parts make subtle, high-pitched whimper sounds*—but no, it was big bro sitting next to me, squeaking his way through a decadent meal served on the yacht deck, prepared by the full-time chef.

Ava's little brother was a very picky eater. He was twelve and hated the delicious food the chef prepared. I was aghast when he constantly demanded peanut butter and jelly sandwiches from the white-coat-clad chef, who begrudgingly complied with the mini millionaire's demands. But Ava and I also took full advantage of the services of the yacht chef. We'd stay up until three in the morning, giggling as only teen girls can do, and then Ava would decide she wanted a chocolate soufflé. We would climb down to the crew quarters of the yacht, which were not nearly as glamorous as the upper decks, and rouse the sleeping chef from his bunk to make us the thing that probably gave him the biggest headache in chef school. I'm sure in those days of soufflé practice, when he was envisioning his life as a chef, he wasn't dreaming of a heady future making PB&Js and three A.M. soufflés for spoiled youths.

#WhyNot **There are glamorous versions of the most generic things. Just like those Versace beach towels with their gold appliqué, you can turn your old sweatshirt into something fit for a yacht.**

DIY Peekaboo Sweatshirt

PREP IT

Sweatshirt

Scissors

Decorative and/or beaded trim/appliqué—go nuts at the fabric store

Hot glue gun and fabric hot glue sticks

DO IT!

1. Lay your sweatshirt flat and cut a scooped piece out of one or both shoulders (I made my sweatshirt asymmetrical, with just one peekaboo shoulder).

2. Cut the decorative trim into pieces, letting the design dictate your cuts.

3. Plan the layout of your trim pieces to edge the cut opening on your sweatshirt shoulder. (I layered three different decorative trims, starting with the largest and ending with a beaded appliqué.)

4. Glue the trim in place. Tip: Fold a little bit of your trim around the cut edge of your shoulder opening and glue it to the underside of the sweatshirt for a more finished look.

Chapter 17

I USED TO BABYSIT MY STEPMOM

She was eleven and I was fourteen and we competed at the same horse shows. I always identified with being a big sister, the nurturing fun type who gives you advice about boys, not the kind to give you a whirly in the toilet bowl.

My future stepmom hung out with a group of young girls her age who would often find themselves in our "tack room"—a glorified horse stall that doubled as our living room at horse shows. They would sit cross-legged on the floor and erupt in naive giggles at my honest anecdotes about preteen life and watch me paint my nails neon green with polka dots. Horse shows drove me crazy because everyone had to wear a "uniform" while they rode. Beyond the almost acceptable knee-high boots, the rest of the polyester monstrosity was my sweaty version of a nightmare. I was known for being a "crazy" dresser at the horse shows. After competing, I'd fly through the campgrounds on my DIY-bedazzled ATV to the tack room and change into something more comfortable. You know, like snakeskin pants or something with a boa and fur.

I have a very specific memory of trying to use my stepmom-in-waiting as my model for a new palette of eye shadow and nail polish I was testing . . . I think it was Urban Decay, to be exact. She was hesitant because her mom was the type who wouldn't let her child paint her nails a shade darker than pale pink—the kind who's perpetually single, lives in Malibu, and sends her daughter to a fancy university in the hope that she'd become a doctor like her. But I was finally able to satisfy my makeover urges when my dad convinced my future stepmother's mom that I was a well-intentioned girl, blue lipstick or no. Ironically, thirteen years later my dad found himself convincing that same mother to give him her daughter's hand in marriage. . . . *Now* who's the bad influence???

I was eventually allowed to put eye shadow and nail polish on my tween step-mother for the first time. Now she buys her own designer beauty products, has a professional makeup artist, and lives in my dad's mansion in Brentwood.

Let me be honest with you. When my dad first told me he was dating Dakota, I nearly puked in my gazpacho. We were at the Grill of Beverly Hills—for some reason he always takes me to a nice restaurant when he has something devastating to tell me, possibly to induce a social muzzle on my instinctive blood-curdling screams. He confessed that he'd run into Dakota at a "club" (yes, my sixty-year-old father frequents clubs—what, yours doesn't!?). He told me they'd started dating and that she had really "grown up" and wasn't "that little girl from the horse shows" anymore. Yup, here it comes again, that bile taste induced by an intense feeling of disgust you can only feel when you realize your father is sleeping with someone younger than you. Apparently, not being that "little girl" also meant she had grown to a towering five-foot-ten, which makes my five-foot-seven father look like an adorable, bald, pony . . . in a custom suit.

I should have known something was amiss when, one morning before the confessional, I arrived at my dad's house to work out on one of his six spin bikes only to find a young blond girl, whom I recognized as one of Dakota's Facebook friends, in his kitchen. My dad told me that he had had a dinner party the night before and the mystery blond was too drunk to drive home, so he let her stay in his guestroom. I was skeptical as I spread vegan butter on my sprouted, fair-trade, fifty-grain toast, because her attitude with my dad was one of extreme familiarity. I had gotten used to my dad having, ahem, interesting taste in women since my parents' divorce ten years prior, but this blond girl was definitely younger than me and she was giving my dad a *suuuuper* hard time about the fact that he didn't have fresh-squeezed orange juice. Like, she was kind of irate about it and had the sort of attitude one might have with a guy friend that you tease, not the dynamic with someone thirty-five years your senior. My doubts grew when I found out later that Dakota had spent the night as well but had escaped in the wee morning hours, probably to avoid confronting scary me and blowing their cover.

Dakota and my father went on to get married* at the Beverly Hills Hotel—not far from the Grill, where my father confessed. Due to my disgust and desire to have a

---

*Shortly before the publication of this book, my dad sat me down in another swanky restaurant and told me he and Dakota were getting divorced. My thoughts drifted momentarily to my now ex-stepmom, whom my future children would never call Grandma. I then replied, "Aww, bummer, Dad! . . . Can you pass the bruschetta?"

functional life, I chose not to attend. You have to protect yourself in life, and if that means not seeing Buzz Aldrin dance at my father's wedding, so be it. My sister went, but she's two years younger than Dakota, so at least she can, uh, look up to her. The wedding cost a whopping 1 million dollars, Dakota wore two different wedding dresses, tons of celebrities watched their first dance, and I heard her nails . . . were a neutral shade of blush.

> **#WhyNot Don't censor your nail color, or you may end up marrying my dad. Test your style limits, fingers first, and try out these easy DIY Beyond Nude Nail Art techniques.**

DIY Beyond Nude Nail Art—Two Ways

Watercolor Nails

PREP IT
White nail polish (optional)

Multiple colors of nail polish

Plastic wrap

Nail polish remover

Cotton swabs

Clear top coat

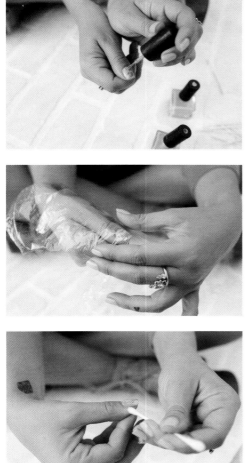

DO IT!

1. If you want the colors to appear brighter, paint your nails with a base coat of white polish and let dry. Then paint dots using different nail polish colors all over your nails, working on one nail at a time.

2. Place a piece of plastic wrap over the wet dots of polish to make them run together, like watercolor paints. Don't worry about getting polish on your cuticles.

3. Clean the excess polish off your finger and cuticle with nail polish remover on a cotton swab.

4. Repeat on all of your nails and seal your nail art with a clear top coat.

Metallic Tape Nails

PREP IT

Base nail polish, color of your choice

Metallic nail tape (see Resources, page 276)

Manicure scissors

Clear top coat

DO IT!

1. Paint your nails with your base color and let dry. I used a taupe color for my base.

2. Lay pieces of the metallic tape down in different directions across each nail. Using manicure scissors, trim the excess tape as close to the end of your nail as possible. Get creative and mix vertical, horizontal, and diagonal stripes.

3. Seal the tape nail art with a couple of coats of clear top coat. Tip: Use a nail file to file down any sharp tape spots after your top coat is fully dry.

Chapter 18

VINTAGE FANTASY

There was a guy in my high school who looked like a Persian James Dean. He was a year older than me, and during his senior year, I asked him to prom.

His name was Danushi, and I immediately recognized his greaser style and brooding demeanor as perfectly 1950s. My love for classic movies made him the ideal candidate for the role of leading man in the melodrama that I believed was my life. I wanted to be his Natalie Wood in *Rebel Without a Cause*. Danushi's hair was styled in a slick pompadour; he wore a white T-shirt with the sleeves rolled paired with Dickies, and smoked Marlboro reds. He barely spoke and preferred to spend his time in the far corner of the school parking lot, tinkering with his slate gray 1983 Crown Victoria, rather than hanging out with any human being. I needed to get under the hood with this sexy loner.

My style tactic was obvious—a teased hairdo, bold red lipstick, and a pair of tailored high-waisted shorts. Less obvious was how I was going to get him to notice me.

I started out by parking near him in the school parking lot. I had just gotten my license at age sixteen and a half, and my first car was a used white Mercedes CLK coupe. I'd get to school early because Danushi was always there, tucked in the back of the parking lot by a tree, smoking a cigarette in the driver's seat of his giant boat of a car.

The first day I parked next to him and deliberately took my time applying my cat eyeliner and putting the finishing touches on my Brigitte Bardot–inspired hairdo, once in a while glancing over at him.

Nothing.

The next day, I parked my freshly washed CLK on the opposite side of Danushi's vintage mobile so that on my way into school I had to cross in front of his car. I looked at him through the windshield and played my best smiling ingenue as I passed. Danushi glared back, exhaling smoke through his nose.

With nothing to show for my style and smile efforts, on the third day I came in like gangbusters. I wore a poodle skirt and walked straight up to his car window and said, "Can you spare a ciggy for this dame?" I instantly regretted the words as they spilled from my excessively red lips.

Danushi looked at me with his strong jawline set in a smoldering line and grunted as he handed a cigarette my way. No words. *Oof, this guy was going to be tough!*

Danushi had only one friend. A far cry from Danushi's vintage perfection, Will was goofy and wore board shorts. After school they would lean on Danushi's car, and I'd hear Will enthusiastically compare a V6 to an inline 6 engine, with subtle nods from Danushi.

That afternoon as I walked back to my car I noticed Will down on his knees studying my tailpipe. He saw me approach and clumsily stood up. "Oh, hey, nice car! Did this tailpipe trim come standard?" Will asked enthusiastically, sipping from his 7-Eleven Big Gulp. I had no idea, but I swiftly responded, "Yeah, totally. It purrs." I trained my eyes to Danushi, who gave me a gorgeous glare.

The dome light in my head went on. "You guys want to take it for a spin?"

"Aw man, fuck yeah we do!" Will yelped and backhanded Danushi in the chest. Danushi coughed.

Danushi turned to me and asked, "Is it manual?"

I was shocked—he had a slight accent.

"No, automatic," I said sheepishly, knowing that driving a sporty car with an automatic transmission was quickly blowing my car-enthusiast front.

Automatic or not, the boys were still down, so we hopped in my car, with Will driving and Danushi in the passenger seat. I sat in the back and stared at Danushi's perfectly combed hair, trying to sniff out his pomade brand—they just don't make guys like him anymore! We tooled around the suburban streets near our school with the guys taking turns driving and testing the acceleration, turning radius, gadgets, and so on. I would have been bored if it weren't for the couple of sideways looks I was getting from Danushi in the rearview mirror.

Over the next couple of months, we became an inseparable trio. I would sit in the middle of the bench seat in Danushi's Crown Vic while he drove and Will sat on the passenger side, all of us smoking. It was mostly just Will and I talking, with Danushi once in a while contributing a grumbled comment. We'd go to the vintage car shows at the diner and have burgers and milkshakes; I fit in perfectly with my beehive hairdo. I'd sit close to Danushi and give him flirty smiles whenever he looked my way. He was growing fond of me—I could tell by the glint in his eye.

One afternoon, while Will was at the dentist and I was helping Danushi clean his leaky heater hose, I worked up the nerve to ask him to prom.

He turned red, kicked at the asphalt, and said, "Okay."

I was elated.

We went to the prom together. He looked dashing in a slim-cut suit and pencil tie. I wore my red lipstick and a dress with a flared tulle skirt. We didn't dance. We sat outside on the hood of the Crown Vic and smoked cigarettes. Toward the end of the night, I leaned over and kissed him. Danushi had obviously never kissed anyone before. He proceeded to eat my face.

With his pompadour flattened and my ruby red lipstick all over his face, I suddenly saw him for what he actually was: a grubby modern teenager.

I was over it after that. The sexy greaser style couldn't mask his teeth kisses. I ended up going after Will, who didn't have the pompadour but made me laugh and didn't bite when we made out.

#WhyNot **Go back to the future with this always-flattering DIY Big and Beautiful Hair.**

DIY Big and Beautiful Hair

PREP IT

Teasing comb

Hair clip

Clip-in human-hair hair extensions (see Resources on page 276, and don't be shy—no celebrity ever has only her own hair on her head . . . don't believe what they say!)

Hair spray

Brush

Curling iron (I like the clipless wand kind; use a wider-barreled curler for a more vintage look)

Bobby pins (optional, if you want to further secure your clips)

DO IT!

1. Part your hair horizontally across the back of your head, about 2 inches up from the nape of your neck, and clip the top section of hair out of the way with the hair clip.

2. Lay out the hair extension pieces. They usually come in two wide sections that have 3 to 5 clips across and four more narrow sections that have 2 clips across. Gently brush out any tangles.

3. Find your second-to-widest strip (it usually has 3 clips across) to clip along your horizontal part. Tease the roots of your own hair before you fasten the extension clip so the teeth have something to grab and the extensions won't slip down the length of your hair as you wear them.

4. Let the top section of your hair down and create another horizontal part farther up across the middle of the back of your head. Clip on the widest strip of extensions (usually 4 or 5 clips).

5. Continue placing 1 or 2 narrow strips on the sides of your head above your ears using the same part, tease, and clip technique as in steps 3 and 4.

6. Tease your own hair at the crown of your head by doing more horizontal parts and teasing each part at the root for some nice, vintage height.

7. To create a more natural look, wrap locks of your hair together with locks of the extensions around the curling iron so they both have the same wave. Brush out the curls for that Brigitte Bardot wave and set with hair spray. Style with black cat eyeliner and false eyelashes!

DO IT Elsewhere! Care for your clip-in extensions with an occasional shampooing, conditioning, and gentle brushing.

Chapter 19
PLAYING DOCTOR

Kids sometimes play doctor, a game disguising the excuse to explore each other's bodies. My first experience with the doctor game was in grade school, when my friend Lizzie and I poured a concoction of dried leaves, sand, and drinking fountain water on our friend Tiffany's vagina to cure whatever made-up maladies she had that day.

Tiffany said she would play the patient, Lizzie was the doctor, and I was the nurse. Our very sanitary exam room was on the ground of the "girls' hideout," basically a hedge that lined the cinder-block wall of one side of the playground. It was enough room for one kid to lay down and two others to loom over her pouring dirt on her vag. It was very clinical.

There are only so many vagina potions you can mix up, so Lizzie and I further explored our own buttholes at her house. Lizzie lived on a farm in the northern San Fernando Valley. She had horses and sheep and a mom who was a news anchor on a local LA TV channel. Lizzie's houseman, a nice Mexican man named Jesus, picked us up in their giant Chevy Suburban, usually used for towing horses, and brought us back to Lizzie's house for after-school playdates. Since Lizzie's mom did the evening news, she didn't get home until late, and Jesus was usually out in the barn attending to the animals, so we had the house to ourselves. There was a floor-to-ceiling mirror in Lizzie's mom's bathroom, a fine 1980s design touch, and we would lie on the floor with our butts up against it, our hands spreading our cheeks and our heads craning around to inquire within. We'd even try to push poop out to see what it looked like. I never could do it, but Lizzie once pooped on the floor, by accident.

After playing pretend doctor with Lizzie, I was shocked when I saw a woman post–plastic surgery for the first time. Lizzie and I were watching *Grease* when her mom walked in looking like she'd gotten beat up, with black-and-blue bruises all over her swollen and stretched face.

"What happened to her?" I whispered, in the midst of pretending I was singing "Summer Nights" to John Travolta.

"She got plastic surgery," Lizzie whispered back, snapping her chewing gum like Rizzo. "The news channel made her do it. She had to tighten her face so she wouldn't get fired."

I was horrified, but quickly got back into singing along with Sandy and Danny Zuko.

My next experience playing doctor had less to do with sandy vagina medicine and was more like a show and tell. I rode the bus to and from my North Hollywood house, which was about thirty minutes away from my Waldorf school campus. It was a tiny bus, for our tiny school, and only about ten kids rode it from grades spanning kindergarten to eighth grade.

My buddy Nicole and I sat near three third graders, upper classmen to us. The two nine-year-old boys liked to pull down their pants and show us their penises. I would turn around in my bench seat so I could peer down onto their tiny wee-wees, which looked like little worms. I remember noticing that they looked different from each other—my first introduction to the circumcised and uncircumcised variety. It was intriguing.

One day the boys claimed it wasn't "fair" that us girls weren't showing them our private parts. They said if they were going to keep showing us theirs, we had to show them ours. They were threatening to take away the peep show.

Ha! My mom had warned me about these impending moments. Private parts were called private for a reason, and I didn't have to show them to anyone if I didn't want to. I refused, and when I got home I told my mom what the boys were doing. I was fine with them showing me their dicks, but as soon as the tables were turned, I turned into a straight-up tattletale.

My mom called the school and the boys' parents to report their inappropriate behavior. I was ostracized from the bus show, but I didn't care—I had my own butthole to look at.

‖ #WhyNot **Doctor up your favorite pair of jeans and take your cute butt out on the town with this super-hip DIY Jean Butt Clutch.**

DIY Jean Butt Clutch

PREP IT

Old jeans (I used a pair of kids' jeans from the thrift store for a smaller clutch)

Fabric scissors

Hot glue gun and fabric glue sticks

Velcro strip

DO IT!

1. Lay the jeans out flat and cut off the legs just above the crotch seam, going straight across. Essentially, you're cutting a really short skirt. Make sure the waistband is lined up and trim it if needed.

3. Flip your jean piece right side out to reveal your jean envelope.

2. Turn the jean piece inside out and hot-glue along the cut bottom edge. Press to create a secure seam along the entire width of the jeans.

4. Create a closure for your clutch by gluing a strip of Velcro along the inside of the opening. Tip: Even if your Velcro has an adhesive back, I highly recommend using hot glue as well to secure it.

Chapter 20
JULIA CAESAR

Every year in high school, the senior class performed a play before graduation. Our drama teacher announced that for our senior play we would be doing *Julius Caesar* by William Shakespeare. Fuck that.

"Excuse me?" I said, as I raised my hand right after he'd made the announcement. "There's only, like, two girl parts in this whole play!"

I had recently discovered my feminist voice, and it was a loud one. I was incensed that he had chosen a play where all the lead characters were men. I had just gotten accepted into college, where I planned to major in film, so I felt justified and determined to have a lead role in the final play of my high school career. My challenge was clear; I needed to play Julius Caesar . . . but as his female alter ego, Julia.

My campaign began, much to the chagrin of my male classmates. There were only twenty-three kids in my twelfth-grade class, and the majority were outspoken dudes who did not want to see me win this part.

"That's not historically accurate," they'd say.

"Your aggression toward women is very historically accurate!" I yelled, pounding my fist on my desk.

With no one being able to make a solid case against it that didn't sound truly sexist, my five-foot-tall, curly-blond-headed self was soon rehearsing the words of William Shakespeare's *Julius Caesar* in my high-pitched voice.

The whole "empress" title was apparently turning me into a tyrant. I assigned myself as head costume designer, but quickly realized I didn't have time to learn lines, make DIY Roman costumes, and graduate with straight As. Like all great leaders, I learned to delegate—I had my mom make the costumes.

My mom has always been an excellent seamstress, and for my Julia Caesar empress costume, she made me a white skirt attached to a white unitard (so it was easy to get on) and paired it with a purple cape with a giant gold Elizabethan collar attached. The kind of collar you'd see Queen Elizabeth I wear in the 1500s, not necessarily anyone in 50 BC, and especially not Julius. But we were already taking liberties with Julius's gender, so why not give him a little flair!?

The problem was that Julia, just like Julius, dies in the play—a violent stabbing murder that required fake blood to get all over my gorgeous costume. We had four performances, which meant my poor mom had to make four of the same intricately designed costumes, but that's how it is when you're the personal seamstress to the empress.

For everyone else's costume we came up with a mix of tunics with rope drawstrings and vests made out of pleather with gold wire-wrapped armbands and cardboard swords.

We performed the play on an outdoor stage that was erected just for the occasion in the center courtyard of our tiny school. I would parade around in my Elizabethan collar, mangling the beautiful words of the Bard, and die at the hands of my pleather-clad classmates, all of them relishing my demise, I'm sure.

"Et tu, Brute?" I croaked dramatically, with Skittle-red fake blood clinging to my unitard, gazing into the acne-covered face of the dude playing Brutus. Falling on the black-painted plywood stairs, I pretended to die and had to lie there as the scene finished. After the first performance, I learned to die in a more comfortable position, using my forearm as a pillow while I waited for the rest of the cast to come pick me up and carry my gracefully positioned dead body off the stage. I was just a real asshole.

I learned a lot from playing Julius Caesar in drag. My feminism has evolved since my teens, and I've found better ways to express a need for equality than sausaging myself into a unitard.

#WhyNot **Play the lead on the stage of life. Express your inner empress with this DIY Wire Scroll Jewelry.**

DIY Wire Scroll Jewelry

PREP IT

Wire, in the metal tone of your choice (I like to use 12- to 14-gauge half-hard wire)

Wire cutters

Pliers

DO IT!

1. Cut a piece of wire using your wire cutters, around 8 inches for a ring and 22 inches for a bracelet, depending on the complexity of the design and your size.

2. Use the pliers and your fingers to spiral one end of the wire a few times. Start small and tuck in the sharp tip.

3. Once the first spiral reaches your desired size (smaller for rings and larger for bracelets) switch directions, creating an "S" curve to add design complexity. Wrap the wire around your finger or wrist to check the size before you repeat another "S" curve in the other direction, creating a mirror image to your first "S" curve and spiral. This second spiral will complete your design, with the other end of the wire at the center of the spiral.

DO IT Elsewhere! Create decorative wire balls using different wire gauges and colors!

Chapter 21

COCAINE ON
THE CARPET

My sophomore year of high school, I had crushes on two different guys: Jeff and Sam. They were seniors and best friends, joined by their shared love of college basketball. The three of us were always hanging out together. They treated me like one of their guy friends, and I enjoyed being the only girl in our trio.

We'd hang out behind the Vons supermarket and look at *Playboy* magazines. I acted like I was totally cool with it. Meanwhile, I was actually bewildered by how different the silicone cantaloupes, pencil-thin eyebrows, and bleached landing strips looked compared to my melted milk duds, bushy brows, and fuzzy downstairs situation. Looking at the glossy pages, I was introduced to the notion of women as objects, and my fledgling feminist was subconsciously born. Later that year I would break both of their hearts.

Our winter break was coming up, and my parents had planned a trip to our Colorado house. They had recently turned their love of skiing into a full-on obsession by building a giant house, ten thousand feet up a mountain. I was allowed to bring two friends with me, and since my parents never said they had to be girls, I invited Jeff and Sam.

"They're sleeping in the downstairs bunk room," my dad said, relenting. "Actually, scratch that—two guys together equals trouble. I want one of them down in the bunk room and one of 'em up in the attic."

"Sure, thanks, Dad!" I said assuringly.

We arrived in beautiful Telluride, Colorado, ready to have a snowy good time. Having a crush on both boys, I thought it unfair to have to decide which one I liked more. I was always one to try to stretch the rules, like the time I brought my cute, furry teacup poodle Gigi to school. She was only two pounds, so I was able to conceal her in a tiny dog carrier and sit her on my lap during class, letting her chew on my finger to keep her quiet. On the third day my school counselor said to me, "You know you can't bring your dog to school every day, right, Kate?" To which I responded righteously, "Would you tell me the same thing if this were my child?"

She looked at me, stone-faced. "Yes."

The first night in Telluride, I snuck down to the bunk room to "check on" Sam, who was bundled in a sleeping bag on one of the giant bunk tiers. I sat near him, allowing my threadbare pajama shirt to hang down and expose my bare shoulder. "It's so cold in here," I said, crossing my arms over my chest and peering at Sam slyly, raising my eyebrow.

He took the bait. "Get in here," he said, peeling back the top of the sleeping bag. I hopped in and enjoyed the warm flannel lining. Sam was a good kisser!

Later that night as I crept back up to my room, I whispered, "Let's keep this between us—I don't want to make Jeff feel weird."

Sam nodded. "Yeah, good idea. Good night, Kate."

The next day we had a blast snowboarding. Sam was always at the ready to help me up after I'd caught an edge. When I complained that my tummy was growling, Sam volunteered to go get me a PowerBar from the lodge.

Boys are so easy.

That night, I told Sam I wasn't feeling well and I went to the attic to visit Jeff. Two birds in the hand are just as good as one in the bush, as my saying goes—and Jeff liked my bush.

Guys always get props whenever they're acting like "players," a.k.a. dating or hooking up with multiple girls, so I guess I was secretly trying on a player identity for size. Don't hate the player, hate the game.

The trip went along smoothly with me enjoying my alternating boyfriends, unbeknownst to them and my parents.

On the second-to-last day of our stay, Jeff told me to meet him in the downstairs closet. My interest was piqued, and I stealthily made my way down to the closet where we stored all the linens. When I opened the door, I saw Jeff *and* Sam sitting on the floor.

Oh no! They must have told each other, I thought. *This is either going to be a threesome or a murder.*

Instead, Jeff grinned at me and pulled out a tiny plastic bag from his pocket.

"Have you ever tried coke?" he asked. I now focused on the bag and saw that it was filled with a fine white powder. I was nervous.

"No," I said, not sure I wanted to try it.

"It's fun!" Sam insisted, crushing up the cocaine on my *Vogue* magazine and dividing it in three lines.

Jeff handed me the magazine and a rolled-up $1 bill. "You first, babe," he said.

"Babe?" Sam asked, looking frantically between me and Jeff, putting two and two together about what I had been doing on our nights off.

Uh oh!

I didn't want to get in the middle of a catfight, so I jumped up, saying something about having to go see what was for dinner, and knocked the lines of cocaine all over the closet's wall-to-wall beige carpet.

"What the fuck!" Jeff exclaimed. I wasn't sure if he was more upset over the spilled cocaine or my betrayal. "This shit was so expensive!" He proceeded to get on his hands and knees, snorting up the cocaine-covered carpet fibers like a pig at a trough. Sam pushed past me on the verge of tears, calling me a bitch on his way out.

Disgusted by Jeff's desperation and Sam's pouting, I went upstairs and plopped down on the couch next to my oblivious dad and stuffed one of my mom's famous powdered sugar cookies into my mouth.

"We're leaving tomorrow, right?" I asked, my mouth full of cookie.

#WhyNot **Be bold and bushy and get what you want with these DIY Bold Brows.**

DIY Bold Brows

PREP IT

Eyebrow brush

Small scissors

Tweezers

Eyebrow pencil that matches the darkest tone in your hair

DO IT!

1. Brush your eyebrow hair straight up with the brow brush and use the scissors to trim the longest hairs so they end at the top line of your eyebrow. Tip: Do this little by little, brushing your eyebrow hairs back in place before trimming more so you make sure you're not taking off too much.

2. Pluck any rogue hairs between, above, or beneath your eyebrows, but be sparing since you want your brows to look nice and full.

3. Fill in your brow with the pencil, creating a square shape at the start of your brows and extending the line down past the tapered end of your brow for a bolder look.

4. Blend in any harsh pencil lines using the eyebrow brush. Wear your bold brows with minimal eye makeup and a bold lip color!

DO IT Elsewhere! Make a DIY brow gel using clear hair gel in a clean and empty mascara tube to further groom your bold brows!

Chapter 22

THE KINDERGARTEN'S ON FIRE!

At the ripe old age of thirteen, my rule-bending friend Leslie brought one of her dad's cigars to school. News spread fast throughout our eighth-grade class that she had something smokable, so by recess we had a group of six kids wanting to venture off for a toke of the stinky stick.

Being the firstborn in my family, and a girl, I was the guinea pig for my father's parental control. My dad possessed a classic "Daddy's little girl" paranoia, and it was amplified by his own experience as a rebellious teen and young adult. While some parents may have gotten caught as teens with a dime bag of weed, my dad got caught with a gallon-size bag of Quaaludes. His cocaine parties were supervised by the likes of John Belushi, so when he sniffed ciga-

rette smoke on my thirteen-year-old self, he probably imagined me hocking hand jobs in the Taco Bell parking lot in exchange for a toke on the crack pipe.

In truth, by this time, I had only smoked a few cigarettes, had just had my first kiss, and wouldn't make it down south to the land of hand jobs for a couple more years. Cigarettes were hard to come by in my small school, and even though

When the idea of me smoking was humorous to my parents

they tasted like kissing my grandpa, they made me feel sophisticated—which wasn't surprising given that my childhood movie choices were highly influenced by my film snob father, who loved classic films that almost always featured a glamorous lady with a coif and a smoke. I even bought a rhinestone-encrusted cigarette holder on Melrose Avenue to elongate my once-in-a-while cigarettes. I guess I fancied myself a thirteen-year-old Audrey Hepburn as Holly Golightly in *Breakfast at Tiffany's*.

In my dad's desperation to keep tabs on my social blossoming, my parents got me a cell phone—a Motorola StarTac, which was straight-up gangsta in 1996! I thought I was really cool with my cigarette holder and cell phone, since no one else in my class owned one. In my fantasy, I was starring in the movie *Clueless*, but in reality, I had been wiretapped.

Since these were the early days of cell phones, the service sucked, especially in the butt-fuck suburbs of the Valley where my school and post-school hangout pads were located. My dad would call me, only to get my voicemail, which would send him into a tailspin of anxiety. His little girl was growing up, and the lack of reliable cell towers was scrambling his only means of control.

The afternoon we went to smoke the cigar, my phone finally worked . . . unfortunately, to call 911.

Bordering our school's kindergarten playground was a vacant lot with overgrown trees, which we decided was the perfect place to hide out and smoke the cigar. It was recess, and we had to move stealthily so as not to attract the attention of the vigilant kindergarten teachers. The high trees sheltered our illegal behavior, and we felt safe to light up.

I was excited to feel like Groucho Marx, puffing clouds of exotic smoke, but none of us knew that you weren't supposed to inhale cigar smoke. We all tried to disguise our coughs and sputters lest we be discovered by the teachers beyond. It was a short-lived attempt, and we decided among ourselves that cigarettes were better. Leaving the lot, dizzy and nauseous, my friend Leslie stamped out the cigar on the base of a tree and left the butt in the dry southern California weeds.

We were heading up the hill to the junior high school when we heard someone yell, "Fire!"

The pack of us preteens turned around to see giant flames leaping up higher than the tallest tree in the vacant lot. I'd never seen flames that big and hot, with black smoke rolling up into the afternoon sky. The kindergartners were quickly being evacuated out the playground gates. We all stood there staring and screaming.

I opened my StarTac and dialed 911, and despite the spotty service, it rang.

I yelled into the phone, "The kindergarten's on fire!"

The fire department had to send a helicopter in addition to trucks to dump water on the fire before it was fully extinguished. Students and neighbors alike came out to gawk. The empty lot was a charred mess, but no kindergartners were harmed. I pulled a Bill Clinton and told my parents I had been in the lot with my friends but I did not inhale that cigar.

That summer, the group of us that had been at the scene of the crime were sentenced to two hundred hours of community service at our school. We had to sand and refinish the wooden jungle gyms, paint the playhouse, and clean debris from the empty lot. I was worried that my association with the reckless fire would spur my dad into even more paranoid control, but to my surprise, he seemed finally at ease—his little rebellious girl was back in the kindergarten playground where she belonged.

> #WhyNot **My days of burning tobacco and kindergartens are over. Contain the flame and make this chic DIY Burnt Paper Art.**

DIY Burnt Paper Art

PREP IT

Picture frame(s)

Basic white paper that fits inside your frame(s)

Lighter

Metal bucket or flame-safe pot filled with water

DO IT!

1. Fold the paper in thirds, then fold it in thirds the other way, creating a small folded square. Tip: If you plan to do a series of these, like I did, try folding each piece a little differently for more variety.

2. Working above the water in the bucket, set the lighter flame to each corner and around the edges of the folded square, just until it starts to smolder and spread. Careful of your fingers!

3. Let the paper smolder a few seconds, then extinguish the flame by submerging the folded paper in water. You might want to practice a few times to find your favorite burned effect.

4. Unfold the paper, let it dry, frame it, and hang it!

DO IT Elsewhere! A flame also comes in handy to seal knots when you're using nylon cord to make jewelry!

Chapter 23
MEETING LEO

My teenage celebrity crushes were: Chris O'Donnell (from his *Mad Love* days), Keanu Reeves (I know, just, what?), Prince William (I could have been a princess, and he likes Kates!), and, of course, my main squeeze, Leonardo DiCaprio (from the thin-face-pointy-chin *Romeo and Juliet* and *Titanic* era). When I was really little, I loved Michael J. Fox in *Back to the Future,* and later in high school it was Justin Timberlake in *NSYNC. I did the typical teenage girl thing where I'd tear pictures of my crushes from magazines and put them on my bedroom wall. I'd dreamily stare at them and imagine my future with them—what it would be like to kiss them, how much they would love hanging out with me. The not-so-typical thing was that I actually got to meet my crushes.

See, that's the blessing, and curse, of growing up in LA and having a connected parent in show business. One time, my dad took me into Michael J. Fox's trailer on the set of *Back to the Future II* to meet him. I don't really remember it, but apparently I just stood there, shocked that he was actually talking to me in the flesh, and then I hid behind my dad's leg because *helllooo*, I was four years old. Were we supposed to do lines of coke and make out!?

I've come to realize that it's better not to meet celebrities. It makes you realize that they're actually human beings who sometimes have sweaty palms and food in their teeth, and also, they don't give a shit about you. Your fantasies of celebrities are always *much* better than the real thing. You meet them, and sure, most of the time they're polite and say hi and thank you when you give them a compliment, but they don't gaze into your eyes and proclaim you are the person they've been waiting their whole life to meet. It's just not that magical, unfortunately. Case in point: when I met the man I believed to be my future baby daddy and perfect mate, Leonardo DiCaprio.

I'd been smitten with him ever since I saw *Romeo and Juliet*. Like the kind of smitten that makes you depressed about how hot someone is and gets your tummy kind of upset when you can't just watch the movie twenty-four hours a day. That puppy love thing that at thirteen and fourteen you think will never pass. My dad knew of my insatiable crush, so he did what any CEO of a showbiz company would do and got us tickets to the *Titanic* premiere, along with passes to the after party.

OooooMG, I was going to meet Leonardo DiCaprio and he was probably going to fall in love with me! I was fourteen and had just sprouted tiny boobs. My nose had grown but my face hadn't caught up, and I wasn't yet sure how to style my naturally curly hair, which had decided to go crazy kinky after puberty. So duh, of course Leo would be smitten with me at first sight. The only question that remained was, *what to wear!?*

Betsey Johnson was the only answer. Her store at the Beverly Center was my mecca for all things funky fashion, and I knew I'd find the perfect outfit to meet my prince. I decided on a shimmery silver slipdress with spaghetti straps, but since I wasn't sure how to rock my new little booby nubs, I also picked a shimmery knit cardigan to wear for warmth and coverage. I completed the look with some black-and-white animal-print platform Mary Janes. I was ready—but so darn nervous—to go watch a movie about people dying on a boat.

My dad hired a car to take us to the premiere of what was at that point the most expensive movie ever made. We found our seats in the theater and I covertly tried to locate Leo in the audience, to no avail. The movie was good, but long, and I was so fidgety watching my future lover on screen, knowing he was in the theater with me at the same time! *Oh,* I thought, *there he is dying a freezing death, but ahhh, he's actually really close to me alive and breathing and probably looking really sexy.*

It wasn't until the after party that I laid eyes on my celluloid soul mate. There was a crowd of people, but I could see Leo's floppy blond hair in between the bobbing bald executive heads. My dad found an executive he knew who was a producer of the movie and introduced me, saying, "She loves Leo, can you introduce us?"

I was starting to feel mortified—this wasn't how meeting him was supposed to go! The crowd was supposed to part in slow motion and he was supposed to spot me, transfixed, as I floated toward him on my animal-print Mary Janes to plant a passionate kiss on his Cupid's-bow pout.

Alas, it didn't work out exactly like that. The producer took us over to the man of my dreams and introduced Leo to my dad first. He looked really cute, although smaller and a little more weathered in real life—dare I say he had a few acne scars and some visible dark circles? I peered out from behind my dad's arm, waiting for my destiny.

"This is my daughter Kate," my dad said to *Leonardo fucking DiCaprio*, gesturing toward me.

Leo turned to me and smiled—a polite smile, an autopilot smile that he probably gave to every other executive's daughter who didn't look like Gisele Bündchen.

"Hi, nice to meet you," he said and stuck out his thin hand.

And we shook hands, mine probably very damp, as I croaked a very unromantic, "Hi, nice to meet you, too."

Then Leo, the man of my many dreams, my Romeo, my Jack, let go of my hand. He turned to my dad, who complimented him on the movie. Leo graciously said, "Thanks a lot," before being tugged by a woman to meet another group of people. He excused himself, still gracious, but not in love with me.

He was gone. I gazed at the back of Leo's head as he proceeded to have the same exchange with another group of people, including two girls around my age, both of them looking expectantly at him with the same expression that was now erased from my face. I knew it was over. I would never be Leonardo DiCaprio's girlfriend, and he hadn't fallen for me as planned. But what was worse, I thought, as I headed home in the car, was that the pictures of Leo on my wall were not going to be the same when I got home. I would no longer gaze at them with the enchantment of our potential future together. Leo had laid eyes on me and turned away; I was not his Juliet after all. It didn't feel good, and what felt worse was delivering the less-than-stimulating story to my girlfriends the next day at school. The whole thing was just *wahh waaahh*.

The good news to come out of this is that fourteen turns into fifteen and finally finds its way to thirty. Leo finds himself a fatter face and an unattractive addiction to supermodels that shows he's not the ideal mate for even the prettiest ladies in the land, and it turns out that he's also really bad at doing accents. I still have a big-ish nose, but my face has caught up and I have my own Romeo now. He may not take poison for me or let go of the broken piece of ocean liner in frozen waters, but his gaze couldn't be torn away by any bald executive, and he makes me quake in my platforms with every true-love kiss.

#WhyNot **I'll always remember shaking hands with Romeo, even though my puppy love was unrequited. Celebrate your puppy love with these DIY Dalmatian-Print Nails.**

DIY Dalmatian-Print Nails

PREP IT

White nail polish

Black nail polish

Scrap paper

Pencil

Clear top coat (optional)

DO IT!

1. Paint your nails with white nail polish and let dry.

2. Drop a little dollop of black nail polish on a scrap piece of paper. Dip the point of a pencil into the black polish and press it into one of your nails to create Dalmatian spots. Repeat around the nail, making your spots sporadic, with no pattern or consistent size so that they look more realistic. Layering a couple of dots over each other can give you those Dalmatian cluster dots.

3. Seal your nail art with a clear top coat to make it last longer, if you like.

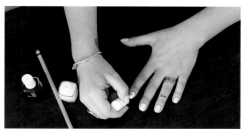

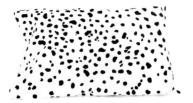

DO IT Elsewhere! Use black fabric paint and a paintbrush to update a white pillow case—Dalmatian-style!

Chapter 24

WASH DOWN YOUR LIPITOR WITH A DOUGHNUT

In a sea of abnormal, there's one family that is the most normal family I've ever met. That family happens to belong to my boyfriend-for-life/husband Joey. They live in Joey's hometown of Indianapolis, Indiana, and his parents—wait for it—are still married! Bob and Sharon have three children, Jennifer, Jason, and Joey (yup, all J names), three grandkids, and a minivan. They go to church, they all eat meat, and they all like each other.

On my first visit to meet Joey's family, I convinced myself that they all disliked me because everything went so smoothly. In my world of "love hard, fight harder," their lackadaisical pleasantness threw me for a loop. I was used to someone either really liking you or really disliking you. Extremes of emotion are my modus operandi, which is why I need weekly therapy. The calm kindness of Joey's family had me convinced that I hadn't met their expectations. Because they weren't fawning over me, I was preparing myself for an onslaught of hate. I cried myself to sleep a couple of nights, driving Joey crazy with my assumptions—he assured me that I was making an ass of us both. It wasn't until I was able to thoroughly psychoanalyze and diagnose my new nuclear family with a healthy set of issues that I felt more comfortable. They had a serious case of normal.

You see, the real culprit is Bob, Joey's father. I love Bob. His good qualities are his generosity, curiosity, and open-mindedness. The things that I, in all my unlicensed, self-appointed psychoanalyst's glory, have deemed Bob's "issues" are as follows: driving, eating habits, and overall stubbornness.

Bob is a scary-ass driver. He insists on driving everywhere we go while we hang on for dear life to the minivan armrests. His usual style is to straddle lanes and check emails while driving, but a good old-fashioned hard-core tailgate is a constant lip-biting favorite as well. Good-natured Sharon has adopted an impressive indifference to Mr. Bob's Wild Ride. She chuckles at our intermittent screeches and my wailings of "Bob, Jesus, you wouldn't have to pull into the emergency lane to risk hitting some-one if you weren't up their damn tailpipe!" Bob's response to our pleas is usually a nasal-sounding, "Welllll."

Bob applies that same "ah, F it" attitude to his cheeseburger consumption. Bob takes medication for his high cholesterol, and he usually washes it down with a milk-shake and a doughnut. The fact that his own mother had open-heart surgery doesn't quell his unabashed denial that he's putting his arteries in a chokehold. I watch Bob dunk his french fries in blue cheese dressing and think of my own dad, who works out ad nauseam and is usually hopped up on the latest pricey fountain-of-youth sup-plements, as if he's Lance freaking Armstrong. Of course, two extremes don't make a right—but how many cattle have to die a cheesy death before Bob gets hip to his health!?

The speeding tickets and cholesterol drugs don't get through Bob's silver-haired head because of his third diagnosed issue, stubbornness. Pleading children and the threat of death aren't enough to make Bob stop driving like a douche because he just doesn't want to. I've witnessed Bob's own daughter say, "Dad, no stimulating iPad games for the one-year-old at nine P.M.!" With little J-name sitting on Bob's lap, blue eyes glued to the retina display, his response is, "Really? That's how I always get him to sleep—now let's search for some monster truck videos." A tantrum quickly follows, from which Bob promptly removes himself while Joey's sister comforts the overstim-ulated child. Bob proceeds to heat up a tub of caramel for his apple slices—"Hey, it's an apple, it's healthy!"

I love my in-laws and they love me. We've established a dynamic that works well for all of us where they happily lead their normal lives and I quietly judge them.

#WhyNot **Put junk food to a better use and make some DIY Soda Bottle–Stamped Pants**

DIY Soda Bottle–Stamped Pants

PREP IT

Pair of pants

Butcher paper or drop cloth

Fabric paint, color of your choice

Paper plate

Soda bottle (preferably a glass bottle with a ribbed bottom)

Paper towel

DO IT!

1. Lay out your pants on a flat, paint-safe surface such as butcher paper. If the pant fabric is thin, place pieces of butcher paper down the inside of each leg to keep the paint from seeping through to the other side.

2. Pour some fabric paint on a paper plate. Dip the ridged bottom of the soda bottle in the paint, just enough to coat it with a thin layer, and dab off any excess paint on a paper towel.

3. Stamp the paint-covered bottom of the bottle all over your pants, dunking it in the paint again as needed. Let the paint dry, flip the pants, and repeat on the other side.

Chapter 25
I WENT TO HOGWARTS

I never learned how to read.

My parents were concerned when, at my ninth birthday party, my friends and I gathered around my one public school friend so that she could read us all my birthday cards. They asked my teacher at the Waldorf School, "Is there something wrong with Kate? When is she going to be able to read?" to which he responded, "Just wait—it's magic."

The Waldorf School, which I attended for fifteen years of my childhood, was a strung-together gathering of trailers deep in the Valley. It was a "private" school, but not of the high-tuition, college-prep breed. It was a place where parents would send their children to have an alternative education, and my parents *loved* to be alternative. Many of my classmates were ADHD outcasts from the public school system who had come there to be embraced instead of ostracized; their hyperactivity being characterized as creative instead of crazy. The culture of acceptance led to me being in a class full of wizards and weirdos who learned to read at their own pace.

Rudolf Steiner was a turn-of-the-twentieth-century Austrian philosopher who developed the philosophy upon which Waldorf education is based. We did have lunch and recess, but the similarities between our school and more traditional schools ended there.

Every day began with shaking my teacher's hand as we entered the classroom. He would greet each of us by name and acknowledge our presence. We stood behind hand-carved wood desks and said the morning poem, which was a greeting to the sun, the moon, and the stars. Then we were sent to get our bag of tiny seashells, which would teach us our daily math lesson.

For each class, all the way through high school, we were given a blank book with unlined pages and a box of colored pencils. Right angles were considered disruptive and harsh, so we would cut the corners off all our papers so that they became rounded. Even our blackboards had wooden surrounds that were made up of every angle except 90 degrees.

We used the blank books with rounded corners as our handmade textbooks. Our teachers would tell us stories about a specific subject, then we would recount the story in our own interpretation and handwrite it inside our blank books. We also drew pictures and decorative borders to accompany the stories. For science classes, we had to actually draw test tubes, contents a-bubbling, and list the formulas in cursive writing with glorious colored pencils.

Our poetry teacher, Diego Montenegro, looked like he had stepped out of 1968 in a wide-brimmed hat and bell bottoms, and sometimes he taught the class in silence. He preferred we call him by his first name. Then there was one teacher, who brought her personal diaphragm to school for us to pass around and study up close. My perspective drawing teacher was blind.

The students had their own quirks. One kid would come to school dressed as a wizard every day. Totally *not* normal, but to us, it became the norm. He would go out in the field at recess with his wand and recite incantations (this was pre–Harry Potter). I'm inclined to think he was the real deal. The popular kids were the ones who were really pro at dancing around the Maypole, and the boys all learned how to knit alongside the girls. It wasn't uncommon to strike up a conversation with your crush while you both sat in craft class proudly knitting or crocheting something out of homespun wool yarn.

Every year we'd have a class called Eurythmy. It's a style of expressive movement that one does to spoken word, all while wearing flowy silk robes. I remember that when new kids came to visit our school to vet it for a day and see if they wanted to make the leap, Eurythmy always freaked them out the most. It's hard to feel cool at thirteen years old, dressed in a silk robe and making wild arm gestures to a German poem. I'm sure they all thought we were in a cult. As a result, there were only twenty-three kids in my grade . . . twenty-three weirdos.

Lo and behold one day, to the extreme relief of my parents, I began to insatiably read and write . . . and I continue to this day, as you can see by the book you're holding in your hands. However, I did have to teach myself to type.

#WhyNot **Piece together your own beautifully weird headboard with no rules or right angles with this DIY Found Objects Headboard.**

DIY Found Objects Headboard

PREP IT

Simple headboard

Variety of hard objects, such as plastic, wood, seashells, ceramic, rope, and so on

Hot glue gun and extra-strength glue sticks

Drop cloth

3 or 4 cans of white spray paint (or the color of your choice—I like white primer because it has great coverage and a matte finish)

Matte spray paint sealer (optional)

DO IT!

1. Lay the headboard flat with the front facing up. Begin by gluing down the largest objects to the top area of your headboard—I used a decorative frame to create an arc in the middle of the headboard and built upon that. Tip: Remember to leave blank space at the middle and base of your headboard for your pillows.

2. Once all the large objects are glued securely, fill in the spaces with smaller objects. I used pieces of rope to create a scrolled border around the objects. Pull or snip off any excess strings of hot glue as you work. Let the glue dry completely.

3. Lay the headboard on a drop cloth outside. Spray-paint the entire headboard white, covering all the objects well. You will most likely need a few coats of spray paint for full coverage. Let dry.

4. Seal with a coat of matte spray sealer, if you'd like, and style in your bedroom!

Chapter 26

A BELLY FULL
OF LIP BALM

My first kiss was on a river-rafting trip in the eighth grade. Mind you, I hate camping and rafting. I'm not sporty, nor am I partial to pebbles in sleeping bags.

Upon arrival at the river, everyone in my tiny class decided to cliff jump. The cliff, which seemed about one hundred feet above the roaring river, was probably a paltry twenty, but I fell prey to the peer pressure and flung myself into the moving current, regretting every second of it. I especially regretted when I missed grabbing the lifesaver ring that the attending bearded mountain man chucked into the water for each thirteen-year-old to grab as we floated by. Most of the kids were grinning from ear to ear, but I was a sputtering mess after swallowing a liter of river water and seeing my life pass before my eyes. *But I've never been kissed!* I thought. I ended up clinging to the second lifesaver (reserved for the children born without the outdoor adventure gene) that they heaved at me farther downstream.

Tom was one of the cool kids, which wasn't saying a lot in a group of twenty-three eighth graders, but I liked him, and rumor had it that he fancied me. The attending parents and our class teacher had a lapse of judgment and let our hormone-charged gaggle set up sleeping bags wherever we wanted in our open-air camp, regardless of coed comingling. Thus, Tom, Tom's bestie, my friend Anne, and I set up in alternating girl-boy-girl-boy order, and Tom was next to me!

I knew this was it. I was ready for my first kiss. Anne was more experienced than I, and she already had an upperclassman boyfriend who had felt her boobies. As I lay on the hard-ass ground, giggling with Tom next to me, I hearkened back to movie kisses—start slow, partially open mouth, await the tongue. The one thing I hadn't anticipated was how fucking long it took Tom to work up the nerve to roll over in his sleeping bag and lay one on me. My freshly brushed teeth were growing fuzzy with each passing minute. I knew I had to have amazing breath for my first kiss, and between my nerves and the passing time, my mouth went dry and I was certain my breath was funky. That's when I remembered the vanilla lip balm!

Duuuhh! In my rolling suitcase—what, you don't bring a rolling suitcase on a camping trip?—I had this exquisite vanilla-flavored lip balm that was the tits! It would totally make me smell and taste amazing, so I whisper-excused myself and shimmied out of my dirt-covered sack. I stealth-ninja'd it over to my suitcase, risking getting eaten by a wolf, or worse, yelled at by a parent, but this was a teen emergency!

Safely back in my fleece-lined envelope, Tom asked me what I just did.

"I was getting a hair elastic for my sleep braid," I lied. Sleep braids were a conditioned necessity on which I was hooked since my youth. When you have long curly hair, you need a sleep braid so you don't awake looking like the Cowardly Lion. I didn't tell Tom about my vanilla lip balm because I knew that would give away my expectations of a kiss. . . . "What are you prepping your lips for, Kate?" I thought he'd ask. So, camouflaged by my lies and the immense dark sky overhead, I proceeded to eat my lip balm.

It tasted really good and it lubed up my dry mouth in a delightful way. But after the fifth or so nervous finger-full, my taste buds were deciphering other flavors beyond artificial vanilla. So that's what poly-paraben-cetyl-isolate and yellow #5 taste like! And maybe it was my nerves, but my tummy was feeling rather queasy.

Finally, after the star-laden sky above us started to glow with early dawn and my lip balm tin nearing empty, Tom kissed me. He placed his sweaty palm on my cheek and kissed my lubricated hole. It was actually a gentle and sweet kiss, and he introduced the tongue with Oscar-worthy timing. I experienced the glorious loin tingles down in the depths of my sweaty sleep sack, and all was right with the world . . . except for the vanilla-scented burp that erupted moments later.

#WhyNot **Have an all-natural DIY Lip Balm Locket at the ready in case you need to lubricate a situation or have a snack.**

DIY Lip Balm Locket

PREP IT

2 teaspoons vitamin E oil

1 teaspoon coconut oil

1 teaspoon beeswax, plus a little extra if you live in a warm climate to prevent melting

¼ teaspoon honey (for sweetness)

A couple drops of vanilla extract or food-grade vanilla oil

Heat-safe measuring cup

Saucepan that's big enough to fit the measuring cup

Wooden spoon

Large locket or poison ring

DO IT!

1. Place all the ingredients in the measuring cup (chip off shavings of beeswax with a sharp utensil).

2. Fill a large saucepan a quarter of the way with water (no more than a couple of inches). Bring it to a boil over medium-low heat and set the measuring cup in the pot of water to create a double boiler.

3. Stir the mixture carefully until it's totally melted. Tip: If you're using vanilla extract, the alcohol base will prevent it from mixing fully with the oils, but the scent and flavor will infuse your final product.

4. Open the locket or poison ring and lay it flat. Pour the melted lip balm mixture into the locket and let it harden. (If your locket won't lay flat, fill one side and wait for it to harden before repeating on the other side.) If you have leftover balm, pour it into an empty mint tin for an easy cuticle moisturizer.

DO IT Elsewhere! Tint your lip balm by adding some lipstick shavings to the mixture!

Chapter 27
LESBI HONEST

Lesbi honest—I kissed a girl and I liked it. Okay, enough of my twenty-first-century pop culture references (*Jersey Shore* and Katy Perry, respectively). Honestly, my first experimentation with the same sex happened at sixteen—I know, you're thinking I got around, but hey, what else is there to do as a teen? School, homework, and carpet munching!

Her name was Kalina and her parents were foreign. She was a beautiful, tall, brunette girl with acrylic nails and a predilection for crop tops. She was known as the bitch in my school, with her haughty attitude and tendency toward judgmental comments. I've always had a thing for outcasts—like a fabulous outfit, they're intriguing because they're different. Kalina was just that, a sassy, low-cut-jeans-wearing loner lesbian who had been out and proud since the age of fourteen. We enjoyed shopping, listening to No Doubt in her Toyota 4Runner, and going to the tanning salon. Kalina was very well groomed and inspired me to get my own set of acrylic nails and use a heart-shaped sticker on my hip when I was in the tanning bed to get a "tantoo." #ugh. We were good girlfriends, like friends who were girls who talked about boys and in her case, ex-girlfriends.

That spring I invited Kalina along on our family trip to stay at our apartment in New York City's Upper East Side. My mom had rented a cute and homey apartment the year prior, in what was framed as an attempt to reconnect with her beloved New York City but was more likely an effort to escape a disintegrating marriage (my parents divorced that summer). I was excited to have a friend along on what would have otherwise been a tense family trip.

I felt so sophisticated with my new lesbian bestie. It was springtime in the city and Kalina and I had a blast hitting up SoHo for shopping sprees and Central Park for laugh-filled picnics. My parents let us go out at night since we were taking cabs, as long as we were back by 12:30 A.M. We ventured to Eighth Avenue, got horrendous fake IDs, and tried to get into a strip club. We were denied by the greasy bouncer, not because he didn't believe our IDs but because the rules stated that all women had to be accompanied by a man. Sexist! I was with a damn lesbian who liked women! I was infuriated at the sexual injustice, and Kalina was a horny lesbian on a mission. We hung out near the seedy place until a suit-wearing man wandered up. We pulled him aside and told him our sad tale. Apparently he saw the opportunity for some tail and gladly agreed to be our male escort into the booby cave.

Inside, I have to say, I was disappointed. I expected a land of lithe ladies with the most perfect perkies you ever did see. Instead, some lady with very visible cellulite was squeaking down a pole, the whole place smelled like a sweaty foot, and the male clientele all looked like my mouth-breathing history teacher.

Kalina and I sat at the bar near a bare wiggling ass and got the scoop from our suited friend. News flash, he was an off-duty cop! I was petrified that I would be delivered back to the Upper East Side in the back of a police car, having to explain to my parents why I was at a strip club next to a pizza-by-the-slice place, but I think Kalina's crop top won him over. He laughed when he heard we were underage and proceeded to buy us vodka tonics . . . which tasted like I was getting a chemical peel down my esophagus. Kalina, of course, sipped like a champ.

With our curfew quickly approaching and against the protests of the creepy cop, I dragged Kalina out by her tiny belt loops and retreated uptown. We walked in and my dad, who had fallen asleep on the couch, asked groggily if we'd had a fun night.

"What did you do?" he asked.

"We saw *There's Something About Mary* on Lexington," I replied, nervously disguising my vodka tonic buzz.

"Oh, that's supposed to be funny," he replied.

"Yeah, oof, was it funny!" I lied, not knowing anything about it. "There's something about her, that Mary," I said as I pushed Kalina into my room.

Kalina flopped on the bed and turned on some late-night channel that was showing commercials for phone sex that were almost more graphic than the strip club we'd just escaped.

We climbed under the spring-weight down comforter, both fascinated by what they could show on TV this late at night. Caught up in our sexually charged night, Kalina leaned over and kissed me.

I was shocked, but whether it was my vodka haze or the girl moaning on the TV commercial, I kissed back.

I'll spare you the details, but we did enough that night for me to inwardly confirm that I am definitely not a lesbian.

The next morning was *suuuuuuper* awkward. We went to breakfast with my family and my dad finally asked, "Why are you girls being so quiet?"

To which I replied, through a mouth full of smoked salmon lox, "We're hungover . . . duh." He glared at us while Kalina cracked up.

"Don't even joke about that, Kate," he threatened.

I rolled my eyes and he went back to eating his spinach scramble.

Kalina leaned over and whispered, "By the way, you're definitely not a lesbian."

I grinned and said, "Phew, I never want to go to another strip club."

#WhyNot **Just like I was a faux lesbian for a night, you can fake a short haircut with this easy DIY Faux Bob Hairdo.**

DIY Faux Bob Hairdo

PREP IT

Hair clip

Bobby pins

Teasing brush or comb

Curling iron

Hair spray

DO IT!

1. Part your hair half up, half down and clip the top half out of the way.

2. Twist a small, flat bun at the base of your hairline and bobby-pin it in place.

3. Unclip the top section of hair and tease the roots at the crown of your head.

4. Use your curling iron to add texture and curls to the top section of your hair.

5. Tuck the ends of the curled top section of your hair in toward your neck and secure them around the bun with more bobby pins.

6. Pull out a couple of pieces to frame your face and spray with hairspray to finish the look!

DO IT Elsewhere! Apply faux half "accent" lashes with lash glue to the outer edge of your upper lash line to amp up your eye makeup!

Chapter 28
CHIFFON SAVED MY LIFE

There I was, my gorgeous chiffon skirt encrusted in cow shit, confronting imminent death.

I decided I wanted to be a fashion designer at the age of nine. I asked my mom to show me how to sew a simple maxi skirt that I could bring with me on our family trip to Steamboat, Colorado. I chose a delicate floral chiffon fabric with pale blue and violet flowers from the fabric store.

As my mom and I put the finishing touches on my stellar skirt design, my three-year-old sister, Tess, wobbled into the room, immediately burst into tears, and de-manded, "*I want one!*" with the urgency reserved only for super-annoying, toddler-age siblings. My mom proceeded to shut her up by making her a matching skirt using the scraps of my fabric. I was livid; mass production is the antithesis of haute couture!

We arrived in Steamboat the next day—I in my skirt paired perfectly with a corre-sponding beaded top and strappy sandals and Tess, ruining my designer street cred, wearing her skirt on her head. She thought she looked great, but I was fuming. Tess had always envied my long blond hair, and in her tiny infant brain, she thought the flowing skirt resembled my luscious locks when worn just so on her baby-haired head.

We spent our time enjoying the quaint town, watching a hot-air balloon show and riding the bus with my grandparents, who always insisted on public transportation. Tess had taken to wearing the skirt-turned-wig every day—so annoying. She even put scrunchies in her skirt hair and wore them out on the town. The bus patrons of Steamboat, Colorado, no doubt enjoyed the entertaining sight of a toddler with a floor-length skirt on her head, the elastic causing her ears to stick out. The grown-ups cooed, "What beautiful hair you have," and I gritted my teeth, irritated that she was getting the attention for my fabulous skirt design. In Tess's mind, she had them all fooled that she had luxurious, floral hair, and in my mind, I had a really dumb sister.

The real reason behind our trip was to visit the land my parents had recently purchased on which they planned to build a new vacation home. In the meantime, my parents had rented the land to a cattle rancher who was using the property to graze his forty head of steer. We all piled in the rental SUV to go see what looked to me like a giant boring field. My sister fell asleep in her car seat with her skirt inching down her forehead toward her eyebrows; she looked like a sleeping werewolf with her very low elastic hairline.

My mom had brought some large rain boots for all of us to wear when wandering around the landscape. I was dismayed by how they paired with my skirt, but I didn't want to step in cow shit in my jellies. Tess awoke, grumpy from her nap, and seeing my bright yellow boots, insisted on wearing a pair as well.

There was an upper plateau where the house was going to be built that overlooked the valley below where the cattle were grazing. My mom wanted to head down from the bluff and explore the valley below. Since Tess was grumpy and far from nimble, with a skirt on her head and my dad's rain boots on her feet, the rest of the family stayed up on the plateau while my mom and I ventured down into livestock territory.

We passed some steer and said "hi." They looked up from grazing long enough to judge that we weren't interesting before plugging back into the long green grass. We kept clumping along in our rain boots toward the stream and marveled at how far away Tess, my dad, and my grandparents were above us on the bluff. At one point, we looked up and they were all waving. My dad even looked like he was jumping—so funny! We laughed and waved back and kept on our merry way. What we didn't realize is that they had a bird's-eye view of the herd of steer and were trying to alert us that the beasts seemed to be merging into a large group and following us.

Finally we noticed that we had company. My mom and I stopped and turned to see the faces of many giant steer trotting in a united front in our exact direction. Their ears were perked up, and if it wasn't deadly looking, it would have been cute. My mom yelled, "Run!" and I hoisted my skirt and took off. The trot turned into a full stampede.

With no trees to climb and the muddy ground swallowing our rain boots, the steer gained on us. My heart was racing. I thought this might be the end—I might just be DOACP: Dead On A Cow Pie. Time seemed to go in slow motion, just like in one of those dreams where you're trying to escape but you just can't run fast enough. The sound of the hooves were thunderous behind us, and I was getting out of breath.

Suddenly my mom stopped. "Do what I do!"

She ripped her shirt off and started waving it over her head, jumping and growling and screaming. I looked down at my small body and swiftly lifted my shit-encrusted chiffon skirt up and over my head and screamed like my life depended on it. Because it did.

The front row of steer looked startled and planted their front hooves, churning up mud and causing the rest of the herd to stop behind them. My mom, seeing that it was working, all of a sudden took off running and screaming straight toward them, and I followed, flailing my little arms over my head and imitating her noises. We had become a pair of scary munchkin predators that sparked an instinctive fear in these giant animals, and the herd dispersed.

We had survived.

We lumbered up the hill to the plateau, periodically stopping and yelling back at the steer to make sure they didn't form ranks again. My dad and grandparents ran to greet us, blubbering that they had seen the whole thing and tried to yell to us and were so glad we were alive! I was so relieved to be away from the killer cattle that I told Tess I'd style her skirt in a top ponytail when we got back to the hotel, and my parents promptly sold the property.

#WhyNot **Save an old bag like my chiffon skirt saved my life with this DIY Ruffled Chiffon Purse.**

DIY Ruffled Chiffon Purse

PREP IT

Silk chiffon, about 1 yard, depending on the size of your purse

An old clutch or envelope purse

Hot glue gun and glue sticks

Scissors

DO IT!

1. Cut a slit 1 to 2 inches wide on one edge of the silk chiffon fabric and tear the rest of the way down to get a strip of chiffon with a raw edge on each side. Repeat until you have a bunch of strips.

2. Start your first rosette by placing a dot of hot glue directly onto the old purse and attach the end of one strip of chiffon. Spiral out from the center point, adding glue as you go.
Tip: Gather the chiffon in little puckers before you glue it down to get that crinkled flower look.

3. Repeat step 2 until your entire purse is covered with chiffon rosettes.

4. Trim any long loose threads, but leave the frayed edge to add design complexity. Pair this purse with all your dressy ensembles!

DO IT Elsewhere! Add chiffon ruffles and rosettes to update an old sweater!

Chapter 29

KEEPING UP WITH THE KARDASHIANS

There's nothing rich people love more than owning horses. I mean, you can't put an Hermès saddle on a hamster. When I was a preteen, we moved to Hidden Hills, a gated community outside of Los Angeles where every other household had horses in the backyard. Our close neighbors were the Kardashians (who didn't have horses in their yard, but their asses were the size of a small pony's), and in true *Keeping Up with the Kardashians* form, my parents decided it was a great idea to fly five horses from the lush Irish countryside to live in the desert landscape of our southern California backyard. That year my parents had gone on a riding trip around Ireland and loved it so much they wanted to re-create it stateside. The horses had to fly on a cargo plane, so to help with the flight and the adjustment to a new continent, the people who sold us the horses sent a nineteen-year-old girl named Fiona to show us how to care for the five giant beasts. She lived in our guestroom and shared a bathroom with six-year-old Tess. I was twelve, and as excited as I was about my new chore of shoveling horseshit, I was more into our version of an exchange student and my high hopes that she would become like an older sister to me . . . *hellllo* sleepovers!

Fiona was a fish out of water in Hidden Hills among movie stars and to-go sushi. She had grown up in rural Ireland and had never been outside the country. Her diet consisted of blood sausage and beer, so my mom's tofu stir-fry and Hansen's sodas took some getting used to.

I became hyperfocused on Fiona's intense need for a makeover. I was shocked that at nineteen she had never worn makeup! At twelve I was already proficient in the art of mascara and bronzer application, and I was excited to exercise my new-found abilities on her beautiful pale Irish skin. But Fiona was a tomboy through and through and resisted my advances, much to my dismay. "This is not what sisters do! There's more to life than horses!" I muttered, seeing myself as her fairy glam-mother and her as my Cinderella in chaps. Rather than hanging out with me, Fiona chose to spend all her time with the horses, and the wedge grew between us, as did my general disdain at her penchant for sweatshirts.

Maybe it was revenge for my constant badgering to pick out her outfits, but in addition to riding my large pony, Charlie, Fiona would make me ride Tess's small spitfire Irish pony, Mickey, to exercise out his crazy energy before my sister could ride him. I know it's every little girl's dream to have a pony, but this one was a little shit! I hated it because as small as Mickey was, he scared me. He had a mind of his own and would take off galloping uncontrollably, or buck in an attempt to get me off his back. I dreaded those afternoon rides on Mickey and would much rather have been experimenting making Gwen Stefani horn pigtails on Fiona's long dark hair.

One afternoon, I was exercising the devil pony when he took off running. Ignoring my yanking on his mouth with the reins, he sped up, then stopped short and pulled his head down, causing me to topple forward and break my arm as my body hit the desert soil below. Fiona was standing in the middle of the horse ring "supervising," and there I lay, with Mickey proudly nibbling a nearby cactus and my arm flapping in

Me and the devil pony Mickey, here dressed as Rudolph for the annual Hidden Hills holiday parade

the breeze. Literally, I lifted it up and saw that my elbow was dislocated, causing my forearm to wobble in the air in a grotesquely detached way.

Fiona was freaked and ran to get my mom, who drove me to the hospital. My grandma was in town and came with us, muttering to Jesus the whole ride there. At the hospital they pumped me full of Demerol, re-set my arm, and put on a hideous cast to help heal the broken bone. It wasn't even a cute cast where I could pick the color and get people to sign it. It was just a giant support with an Ace bandage wrapped around the entire length of my bent arm. I also had to wear a navy blue sling that gave me dreadlocks in my hair from the neck strap. It was my right arm, and I'm right-handed, so I was forced to write, draw, and, worse, apply makeup with my clumsy left hand. The only positive was that my doctor swore me off riding until I was completely healed—I was safe from the tiny devil pony and Fiona's lessons.

I focused on recovering, and Fiona made friends with our twenty-two-year-old nanny, who took her out to bars. I was jealous and looking forward to her exit back to Ireland. In my one-armed misery, it became my preoccupation to tarnish her reputation with my parents. I spied on her and discovered she was sneaking cigarettes in the barn. Afterward she would go straight to the bathroom she shared with Tess to wash her hands and brush her teeth. I reported it to my mother, who shrugged and said, "What do you want me to do about it? She's nineteen, she's legally allowed to smoke."

"She could catch the whole barn on fire!" I yelled, gesturing with one arm. "Hellllo, hay is like, the most flammable!" But to no avail. My mom didn't want to embarrass Fiona by confronting her bad habit and told me to mind my own business.

Fiona kept in my parents' good graces, the horses adjusted to their new hot and dry California landscape, and then it was time for Fiona to go back to Ireland. My arm was almost healed, but I still gave her a one-armed hug good-bye. Our relationship was never the sister, makeover, watch-*Dawson's-Creek*-together bond that I'd hoped for.

After Fiona was gone a couple weeks, I was searching my sister's bathroom cabinets for a hair elastic when I happened upon a half-finished forty-ounce bottle of malt liquor. The last of Fiona's stash! She had been sneaking drinks of warm malt liquor in a six-year-old's bathroom! I was disgusted, and disappointed that I hadn't found it earlier.

"Mom!" I yelled. "Get in here!"

#WhyNot **For me, the luck of the Irish was a whole barn full of horseshit. Hopefully one of these delicate DIY Horseshoe Necklaces will bring you more luck than the Irish sent me.**

DIY Horseshoe Necklace

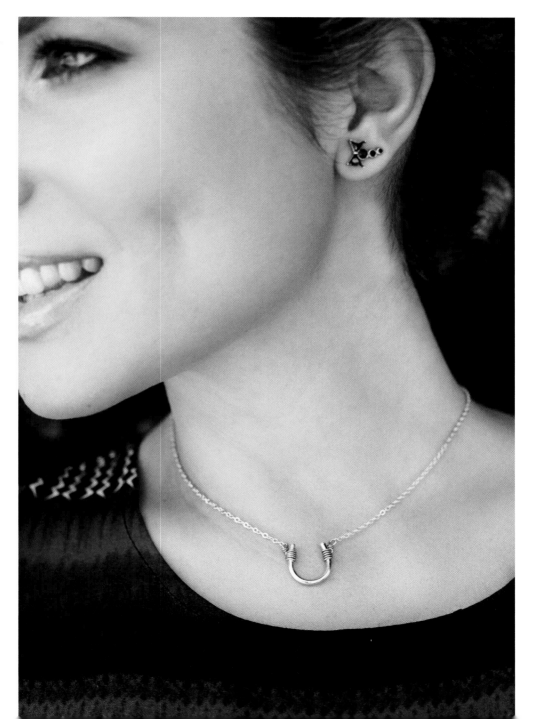

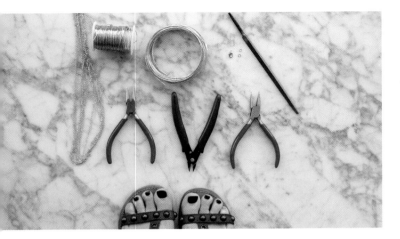

PREP IT

14-gauge half-hard wire

Wire cutters

Metal file

Delicate chain

28-gauge thin soft wire

2 pairs of pliers

2 open jump rings

Clasp

DO IT!

1. Bend the 14-gauge wire into a horseshoe shape and cut to the desired pendant size.

2. File down any sharpness on the tips of the horseshoe pendant using the metal file.

3. Cut a piece of chain to the desired necklace length, then cut it in half so you have two equal lengths.

4. Cut a 6-inch piece of 28-gauge thin wire and wrap it a few times around one tip of the horseshoe pendant. Twist the two ends together with the pliers to hold secure. Trim one end of the 28-gauge wire and tuck the sharp tip into the twist using your pliers.

5. Using the long remaining piece of the 28-gauge thin wire, stick it through the bottom link of one of your chain pieces and twist it into a loop to securely attach the two. Trim any excess thin wire with your wire cutters.

6. Repeat steps 4 and 5, connecting the other chain piece to the other tip of the horseshoe pendant.

7. Using the pliers to open and close the jump rings, attach one jump ring to each free end of the chain and then a clasp to one of the jump rings to create a closure for your necklace.

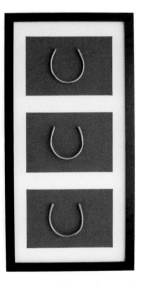

DO IT Elsewhere!

Make horseshoe wall art using 10-gauge wire horseshoe shapes hot-glued to a paper backing inside a picture frame!

Chapter 30
PACK YOUR BAGS AND WEAVE

I was getting ready to move from LA to Santa Barbara to attend UCSB, and I wanted a new and different look for my freshman year of college. I was sick of my growing-out pixie cut, which was now a layered bob verging on old lady 'do. I wanted longer hair but had already tried extensions to match my hair texture, and it looked a little too Lady Godiva. My solution? Braids.

I'd always loved the tiny braided extensions that black girls wore, and I figured that hairstyle would be the perfect way to have long hair while disguising the short length of my actual hair. But how to get them?

The manicurist at my hair salon told me to call her sister Toni. Toni did hair out of her house in Compton (sometimes known as the "hood" in South LA). I was told she was a really good braider and could handle my short (white girl) hair. I was so excited and called her right away to set up an appointment. I told her I wanted braids all over that were really long and really blond.

I showed up at Toni's ground-floor apartment, which was protected by a barbed wire fence. I parked my Mercedes coupe on the street, already getting some skeptical looks from the neighbors, and knocked on the iron security door that was Toni's front door.

Toni was delightful, very warm and welcoming, and immediately started inspecting my hair.

"It's short!" she said, running her fingers through my curly coif. "And so soft, but I can do it—I got quick braidin' fingers."

Toni ushered me to the salon chair that was in the middle of her living room, facing the TV. There was one glaring overhead light and a small side table holding plastic packages of platinum blond hair.

"Oh, it's synthetic?" I asked, inspecting the hair packages.

"Yes, sweet girl, that's how it's done!" Toni said, raising her eyebrows at me. "You want that really tiny microbraid look, you need the fake hair so we can seal it and it won't unravel. The only thing is, you can't use a curling iron on it 'cuz it'll melt . . . like Barbie hair." I'm assuming that was her trying to speak my language. It worked, because every girl knows you can't curl Barbie's hair without it melting off. So sad.

"Huh, okay," I said, trusting her because she was obviously the expert. I plopped myself in the salon chair, ready to become Bo Derek.

There was no mirror, just the TV in front of me, so for three hours I sat watching daytime talk shows and once in a while chatted with Toni as she tugged away at my hair. She'd comb it, part it, grab a tiny section of the long, synthetic blond strands, and braid them in with my hair. I felt the little braids hit the side of my face as she finished each one, and I could inspect them up close. They were tiny, each one about an eighth of an inch wide and really long. Toni wasn't kidding—she had those braidin' fingers!

About four hours into the braiding, Toni's boyfriend came home with her five-year-old son. The kid sprawled on the floor and watched some TV until his grandma came to pick him up. Toni's boyfriend went and got her takeout food because the hours were ticking by.

About six hours into braiding, Toni had eaten her lunch and was starting to complain about her stomach hurting. I could hear it growling by my ear as she stood near, braiding and braiding. Suddenly Toni stopped braiding and ran to the bathroom and threw up. She'd gotten food poisoning from the takeout!

I felt so bad for her; she was sweating and looking really ill. I offered to leave and come back the next day.

"You can't leave!" Toni exclaimed. "You got half a head done. I can't let you walk outta here like that!"

So I stayed in the chair, staring at the TV with Toni once in a while retreating to the bathroom. It was like the Olympics of hair braiding. She would *not* give up just because of an injury—she was a champion!

Thirteen hours after I got there, my braids were done. I never officially counted them, but there were certainly hundreds of tiny platinum braids all over my head. I finally caught a glimpse of myself in the mirror and was aghast! The braids were stiff and splayed out like something from a Tim Burton movie. Toni saw my horror and laughed.

"Don't worry, sweetie! I haven't dunked 'em yet!"

"What?" I asked. I had no clue what she was talking about.

"Ya gotta dunk 'em in boiling water to smooth and seal the braids," Toni said, bringing over a pot of water to the kitchen table.

I stood over the steaming pot, and she dunked chunks of my synthetic braids into the hot water, which did indeed smooth them to Bo Derek sleekness.

Holy crap, I loved those braids! I left Toni's house after our very long day together, wished her well with her E. coli, and flicked my intricately long tresses all the way back to my car, which was still there.

When I arrived at college, UCSB did not know what to do with me and those braids. I got so many incredulous questions from my fellow white girls. . . .

"Is that all your hair?"

"How did you do that?"

"How long did it take?"

"Can I touch it?"

I also found that I got new attention from a whole different demographic of guys. I thought it was because I was so funky, but it was more likely because I looked like a stripper. The platinum was very shiny and the braids reached my lower back. Guys probably thought I moonlighted as Doe Bareback, the pint-size pole dancer with butt-length braids.

I followed Toni's haircare rules to a T. She had instructed me to do the "weave pat" if I had to itch my head. No actual fingers digging into the braids, because it would break the hair and make them frizzy. So every time I had an itchy head, you'd find me hitting myself with the palm of my hand. I also wrapped my hair with a silk scarf every night to keep the braids smooth—the friction from the pillow would make them fuzzy. Before bed I would carefully wind my scarf around my head and fasten it with a knot at my forehead. I looked like Bret Michaels meets Aunt Jemima.

After nearly three months, it was time to take out my braids. They had grown out too much at my scalp, and I was looking a little ragtag. It took me almost four hours to unwind all of the braids that Toni had expertly woven. When I finished, there was a pile of crimped synthetic hair on the couch next to me, and I looked like Albert Einstein, with the craziest crimped blond Afro.

Gone were my sassy Bo Derek days, and I was back to being a college freshman with an old lady bob who rode a spray-painted pink bike to school.

I miss those braids. Next time I have thirteen hours to spare, I'll probably get them again. I wonder if Toni is still around.

> **#WhyNot You may not have thirteen hours to spend getting Bo Derek hair, so here's my quick-and-easy DIY Braid Crown, which will make you feel just as queenly.**

DIY Braid Crown

PREP IT

Teasing brush or comb

2 clear hair bands

Bobby pins

DO IT!

1. Tease the roots at the crown of your head for a more romantic look.

2. Braid your hair in two pigtails positioned above your ear and use the clear elastics to bind the ends. Tip: If you have really long hair, put the pigtails closer to the back of your head, still above your ear line. If you have shorter hair, position them closer to your temples and above your ear line.

3. Crisscross the two braids across your forehead or the top of your head, finding a look you like, and bobby-pin them in place. Tuck in the ends of each braid to conceal them.

4. Use the pointed end of the teasing comb to gently loosen the body of each braid for a fuller and more disheveled look.

DO IT Elsewhere! Braid three pieces of jute twine to create a whimsical curtain tie-back!

Chapter 31
HELL IN PARADISE

For my mom's sixtieth birthday, she gave herself a three-week trip in a private villa on the island of Capri, Italy. Let me tell you a little something about Capri . . . it's paradise. An Italian paradise complete with hillside mansions overlooking the sea, beds with cascading canopies, cobblestone streets leading to a quaint town square, pasta for days, and A-list neighbors like Leonardo DiCaprio (enjoying his island of origin) partying next door.

Joey and I committed to coming for the full three weeks, which was the longest vacation I'd taken since never. We had considerable anxiety about being away from work—we had recently joined forces to run the Mr. Kate business together, and entrepreneurs never rest! But my mom promised excellent villa Wi-Fi and I knew I'd get some amazing photos for the blog. My little sister, Tess, came as well, and we were all set for a gorgeous, relaxing vacation, counting on the claim that any carbs consumed in Italy won't make you fat.

After the boat ride from Naples to Capri and a petrifying drive up the mountain to the hillside village of Anacapri, we arrived at our Italian dream pad. The open-air house had Old World charm and organic gardens. The tiered tiled patios gave way to a pool that overlooked the Mediterranean below. The blue-and-white-tiled kitchen opened up to a giant table for eating al fresco in the sea breeze. All was well with the world, until Sven and Ted showed up.

My mom had met Sven and Ted, a wealthy East Coast married gay couple, on one of her extravagant cruises in some far-off land. Since my parents' divorce, my once socially skeptical mother had become a huge fan of giant boats and communal dining. Her state-room suites would take her away from her problems, finding her equally wealthy and flailing friends plus bonus flings with crew members. Sven and Ted had been together for thirty years. Ted had hit a stretch of bad luck twenty years prior when he was in a car accident that killed his parents and put him in a coma. He recovered, only to get hit six months later by a bus that paralyzed him on one side of his body. Sven was his caretaker, who loved to drink and hook up with Filipino cruise waiters while indulging in Ted's disability checks and trust fund, and had become BFFs with my mom.

When Sven and Ted showed up in Capri, my sister and I gave each other a knowing glance and braced ourselves for a wild ride.

Sven flitted about the villa, mixing anyone who blinked a vodka, *limoncello*, or whatever . . . and my mom blinked a lot. Sven also made friends with all the town randoms, and all of a sudden villagers were stopping by the villa to hang by the pool, eat our antipasto, and speak no English.

Ted liked to massage shoulders. His paralyzed right arm, which he kept tucked in his pants pocket, had enabled his left arm and hand to reach Hulk-like strength. He was partial to walking up behind Joey seated on the veranda and laptop-focused to give him an impromptu, he-man, trapezius squeeze that would make Joey squeal in pain . . . but it's hard to say no to a paralyzed masseur.

All of this sounds harmless enough, except for the fact that Sven hated my sister. He called her a brat and was a broken record with his prediction that she would never find a husband to "put up with her shit." This was insulting to her, and in defense of my little sister, we both shunned him as only two sisters can do to a drunk housemate in paradise.

One night all the kids—and by kids I mean the people in their twenties, who were more mature than the fifty- to sixty-year-olds—decided to take a break from paradise and visit nearby Positano for a night. I know, tough. Excited that the "kids" were out of town, Sven and my mom threw a rager. All the villagers came to the gated villa for a toga party. Sven spent the night inspecting men's packages under their togas, and my mom had sex with someone in the pool.

The morning after, we kids returned to a trashed villa and some very hungover old people. Ted was pissed about Sven's wandering boner and banished himself to their room to pout. Oblivious to the mess they had left, my mom and Sven napped off the previous night on the striped pool chairs while Tess and I were left to mop the sweat and vino off the villa floors. Paradise lost, the battle had been waged, pinning my mom and Sven against two fed-up daughters.

Later that night I was brushing my teeth when an inebriated Sven appeared in the bathroom door.

"What's your problem?" he slurred. "You're such a bitch to your mom! She's just trying to have fun, and you and Tess are acting like spoiled brats!"

This was not the time to throw insults at me; I'd just fished a bed sheet out of the pool. I wheeled around, brandishing my toothbrush as a weapon and splattering Tom's of Maine in his bloodshot eyes.

"Don't fuck with me, Sven!" I growled. "I am in no mood." (I'd always wanted to say that—it sounded so British!)

My intensity must have rattled his vodka-soaked soul, because he glared at me and stomped off. I retreated into the bedroom, where Joey said, "What the hell was that about?" I crumpled on the bed underneath the beautiful cornice canopy and mumbled through my toothpaste-crusted lips, "I didn't get to rinse."

The next day we all fled Paradise. On the boat ride back to the solace of real life, my mom ignored us, Sven puked over the railing, Ted massaged Joey's shoulders, and Tess and I did a happy jig that we were done with this vacation.

#WhyNot **You don't have to leave the safety (and sanity) of your home in order to experience paradise. I much prefer a basket canopy to a basket case. Create a dreamy DIY Basket Canopy to make any bed villa-worthy.**

DIY Basket Canopy

PREP IT

About 4 feet of ½-inch-wide natural fiber rope, like Manila or sisal

Large natural-fiber woven basket—preferably one with no handles

Scissors

Hot glue gun and extra-strength glue sticks

2 to 4 lightweight curtain panels, depending on the size of your basket

Large screw hook with anchor for hanging, like Cobra Anchors for ceilings

DO IT!

1. Tie a large knot at the end of a piece of rope—err on the side of longer so you have slack to hang the canopy at your desired height. You can always trim it later.

2. Push the rope through the center weave at the bottom of the basket, letting the knot act as a stopper. Tip: Depending on the weave of your basket, you may need to jab a little hole with scissors or a knife to be able to fit the rope through.

3. Hot-glue the top of the curtain panels along the inside rim of the basket, making little pleats as you go for a more gathered look.

4. Mount the screw hook in the ceiling above your bed or daybed. Tie the rope around the screw hook or a tree branch outside to hang the basket canopy. I styled my basket canopy with some vintage chandelier crystals hung along the rim of the basket.

DO IT Elsewhere! Turn a wire basket into a light fixture by using a lightbulb cord kit!

Chapter 32

SANTA'S ON RETAINER

Santa and I got along great. I was usually pleased with his ability to heed my letter requests and leave a mountain of gifts under the tree. To return the favor, I generally behaved myself throughout the year, and every Christmas Eve I left him organic, agave-sweetened cookies to help with his carb addiction.

One year, my big wish for Santa was to make my American Girl doll into a real person. Her name was Felicity, she had red hair, and she was my favorite. I had cute outfits for her, a canopy bed, and this weird thing that looked like a frying pan with a lid that supposedly warmed her feet in the olden days (where she was from). We were tight, like besties, and I wanted her to be able to walk and talk with me. I knew it would be the perfect situation, and Santa would definitely be able to grant me this wish.

That Christmas Eve, I tucked Felicity into her mini bed, gave her a kiss, and told her she'd be alive in the morning. I was so excited.

I awoke the next morning and rushed to her bedside, ready to have my first-ever convo with my living doll. Fucking Postal Service! Santa had definitely not gotten my note, because we were bros and I know he wouldn't have left me hanging, but there was Felicity, stiff and lifeless, just as I had left her.

I spent the next year getting over Felicity's non-human-ness while also cultivating a deep knowledge of the world's postal delivery services. I ultimately decided USPS was too pedestrian, and honed in on FedEx, which had tracking numbers and express delivery that would surely not fuck up my North Pole correspondence. Just to be sure, I started sending my letters to Santa in July.

That year, Felicity started getting on my nerves, and I decided I wasn't going to waste my big wish on her life. I had a much more important request for Santa—I really wanted a retainer.

I was in fourth grade and Hailey, the prettiest girl in my class, had a pink retainer. I was insatiably envious. Hailey would pop it in and out of her mouth and make it look so darn cool. I wanted to feel what it felt like to have a bright-colored metallic thing perfectly nestled around my teeth. I had made my mom take me to the orthodontist, hoping he'd find an imperfection in my annoyingly straight teeth. In the examining chair, I purposefully tucked my lower jaw back to try to fake an overbite, but the orthodontist didn't bite. I left with no retainer and a hollow place in my soul.

I took to faking a retainer by using the round foil from large chocolate coin candies. I molded the soft aluminum to the roof of my mouth and over my front teeth. I was still unsatisfied by my DIY retainer attempts until I realized that Christmas was around the corner. Santa was my only hope! If he could slide down chimneys with that fat ass of his, he could definitely get me a real retainer.

I wrote "a retainer" at the top of my wish list that year and awaited the blessed day.

Christmas morning was upon us, Baby Jesus was sleeping on some hay, and I was about to have some metal in my mouth. As I made my way through the pile of wrapped gifts, I was pleased to discover that everything else on my list was there—FedEx was absolutely the right decision.

Me; my little sister, Tess; and our two lifeless BFFs, enjoying a day out on the town

I was salivating as I unwrapped my last gift, a small box, the perfect size for a delicate dental appliance. I could almost taste it. My excitement quickly turned to an uncontrollable rage as I opened the box to reveal a goddamn miniature tea set for fucking Felicity. That bitch. What the fuck?

I crumpled in a dejected ball on the shards of wrapping paper.

"What happened, Kate?" my mom asked.

"He didn't bring me a retainer," I answered, super depressed.

"Maybe it's because you have perfect teeth and he doesn't want you to ruin them with a retainer," my mom cajoled, but it didn't soothe my pain. A retainer was my ticket to a happy life.

Having experienced soul-crushing disappointment two years in a row, I swore off Christmas and thus began a future of misanthropic Decembers.

Twenty years later, Santa, Felicity, and their friend Baby Jesus had the last laugh. I was diagnosed with TMJ . . . and got a goddamn retainer.

#WhyNot **My predilection for metal appliances has moved away from my mouth and onto my shoulders. You don't have to rely on Santa or visit an orthodontist to rock these sweet DIY Barrette Epaulettes.**

DIY Barrette Epaulettes

PREP IT

Jacket, preferably one in a sturdy fabric like denim

Metal barrettes

Hot glue gun and glue sticks

DO IT!

Plan the barrette layout on the shoulders of the jacket, making sure they will lie flat, and hot-glue them in place.

DO IT Elsewhere! Fasten barrettes around a wide belt to give it removable metal embellishments.

Chapter 33
MILLIONAIRE MOTEL

The end of the winter marked the start of horse show season. For my family this meant that every Friday after school, the four of us—Mom, Dad, Tess, and I—would all pile into our red Dodge Durango and drive three hours to the desert show grounds in Palm Springs, where we'd spend the weekend competing in various horse jumping competitions. My once-health-food-Nazi mother had been worn down by my parents' freezer-burned marriage, giving her a "fuck it" apathy that meant our Friday night meals on wheels were usually drive-thru fare. My sister, Tess, and I loved it. We'd pass out in a carb coma, only to be awakened upon our arrival to the Ritz Carlton where all the families stayed during the horse show.

Come Sunday evening, tired and sunburned from the weekend's competitions, we'd check out and pile our riding boots, show clothes, and luggage into the Durango and make the trek back to LA. By year two, my mom had become weary of constantly checking in and out of a hotel's front desk. Her solution? We'd stay at a much cheaper roadside motel instead, but rent the room straight through for six weeks so we could keep our clothes there and just show up already settled.

My sister and I were pissed.

"Who are we going to hang out with?" I whined.

"They don't even have room service!" seven-year-old Tess cried.

To ease our apprehension, Mom told my sister and I that we could decorate the motel room any way we wanted and make it "our space." This prospect excited me so we headed to Kmart.

It's hard to find a more expensive hobby than English equestrian competitions. Many of the families that participated were legit billionaires. There was the Levi Strauss family, the Firestone tire family, the Dillard's department store family, the Campbell Soup family, and us, the family of heathens who ate french fries from the drive-thru and lived at Cactus Jack's Motel for six weeks.

Of course, the horses themselves were part of the expense. It was totally normal to drop four years of Ivy League tuition on a small pony not much bigger than a Great Dane. Six- and seven-year-olds paraded around on their $300,000 pets with trainers and groomers in tow. There were even professional braiders who made their living creating pageant-worthy hairdos on the horses.

Tess and I were not exempt from this excess. My parents didn't have the wealth of the likes of Levi Strauss, but Tess had some very pricey ponies, and one of my horses cost $80,000. My favorite horse was my jumper Shorty, who was a steal at thirty grand. We slept at a grimy motel and awoke to ride animals the price of some houses—a rich person's paradox spearheaded by my weird mom.

Back at the motel, I had come up with the perfect design scheme. I decided to go for mixed animal prints and red patent pleather. I was fourteen years old and didn't realize that I was going down the polyester path to making our motel room look like a bordello. We unpacked the two zebra-print rugs, multiple red feather boas, and sequined bedspreads and throw pillows. I got busy decorating our new temporary housing and hung the boas around the headboards, dressed the beds with new comforters and pillows, and placed the rugs just so to cover the horrible motel carpeting. I accented the dressers and nightstands with shiny trays and tacked printed placemats over the beds as wall art. When I was finished, it looked like a really homey, albeit glitzy, hooker's den.

I thought it would be a great idea to throw a housewarming party to show off our new digs. Mom happily obliged. I went to work party planning. Mom was to be the chef, and we designed a menu of Crock-Pot spaghetti Bolognese and George Foreman Grill–pressed paninis. My sister was in charge of mixing the drinks, which consisted of a virgin cocktail of one part Pellegrino and one part pineapple juice. Dad was responsible for the entertainment, and he played his favorite Sinatra CD on the boom box. I planned the evening's activity, which was tie-dying our bath towels and bedazzling our television remote.

The party was a smash. All five of our friends came, and Cactus Jack's parking lot would never again see that many Bentleys.

That would be our only year at Cactus Jack's. The next year, my mom rented an RV.

#WhyNot **Take a dingy lamp and make it look like a million bucks with this DIY Mosaic Lamp.**

DIY Mosaic Lamp

PREP IT

Mosaic mirror tiles

Lamp with a base that will easily fit the mirror tiles

Hot glue gun and glue sticks

DO IT!

1. Start hot-gluing mirror tiles in place at the base of the lamp by the cord and work your way around. Tip: If there are any gaps between tiles, you can hide them at the back of the lamp.

2. Continue to glue the tiles in layers up the body of the lamp.

3. Plug in and add a pretty shade!

DO IT Elsewhere! Glue mosaic mirror tiles onto a scrap of leather and connect to a chain with jump rings for a funky necklace!

Chapter 34
MY BIG GAY FAMILY

Homosexuality runs in my family. My grandfather had sixteen siblings, so the odds were that at least a few of them would be born gay.

Back then, in the backwoods of Maine, you gave birth to your farmhands. My grandfather's mother was perpetually pregnant, and the entire family lived in a two-room house where all the children worked as loggers to put food on the table. My mom grew up knowing that a few of her aunts and uncles were gay, but no one from the repressed New England family ever officially came out of the closet.

There was Great-Uncle Freddie, who never married and had seven Chihuahuas. We'd visit Maine and stay with my grandparents during the summers, and Freddie would come over to have some of my mom's delicious clam chowder. He wore Hawaiian shirts, and his fat Chihuahuas wore dresses with gingham aprons and had names like Ida and Nancy. Mom would exclaim to my grandpa, "Dad, Uncle Freddie makes outfits for his tiny dogs—he's *gay*!" to which Grandpa would shake his head and say, "No, he's just eccentric."

And then there was Great-Aunt Deb who wore dungarees and read catalogs about seeds in her downtime. She was an avid gardener with a wicked sense of humor. Deb had never been seen with a man, but she did live with a female "roommate" for fifty years. When Mom was a kid, Deb would take care of her and bring her along to her "friend's" house, where she'd have my mom wait outside while they "took a nap."

Then there's my mom, who comes from a family of seven kids. None of them are gay, but her sister married a gay guy and my mom is a self-proclaimed "fag hag."

My aunt didn't know her husband was gay when she married him. None of us did. And it seemed not to have dawned on the guy yet, either, because this man married my aunt, had kids with her, and then, years later, said, "Oh wait, JK, I'm gay!" (I'm paraphrasing.)

They had been married for twelve years, had three kids and apparently a lot of homosexual friends in Puerto Rico . . . or at least that's how her husband's inbox read when he accidentally left it open one day, and my, were they friendly emails! He's now happily married to his male lover, and my aunt is batshit crazy.

My mom started a talent management company when I was about eight years old managing mostly gay and lesbian comedians and screenwriters. She worked out of our house with her gay business partner, Eric. I loved Eric and took it upon myself to help him quit smoking by flushing all of his cigarettes down the toilet and replacing them with tiny rolls of paper that read inspirational things like, *"I love you Eric, don't die"* and *"Draw a picture on this paper instead of smoking it!"* He would whine that I was wasting his cigarettes, but I think he secretly liked that I cared.

In order to submit their clients for potential gigs and roles, Eric had to constantly make VHS copies of the comedian's acts to send out to casting directors—this was the 90s when there were no DVD burners or handy YouTube links yet. I wasn't allowed to watch TV as a kid but Eric let me sit and watch the acts get copied to new tapes because they had to play all the way through each time to be fully copied. I watched those gay guys and lesbians doing their comedy acts so many times, I knew them by heart and would often relay the jokes of their "coming out" stories to my, not so intrigued, elementary school friends. This was the type of nondiscriminating home life I enjoyed as a youngster.

When I was in my teens, our horse trainer was gay and very flamboyant. He lived up the street from us and would often come over for dinner. On one occasion, when my grandparents were visiting, my rigid German grandfather said something about not wanting "his kind" over at our house. I was usually quietly respectful of his grumpy worldviews but this was crossing the line, I had heard too many coming out stories over and over again on VHS tapes to let that slide so I lit into him saying,

"If you don't like our homosexual friends, you can leave because maybe we don't want *your* kind here!"

Everyone gasped and my mom smugly smiled, proud that she had raised a mini fag hag. Grandpa retreated to his room where he pouted for a few days over my impudence and scorned morals.

I realize the process of acknowledging one's sexuality and then revealing it to friends and family is unique to everyone. I tried hooking up with girls twice in my life, once in high school and another time with my friend in college. Both times reinforced my hetero persuasion, but I'm happy I allowed myself the experimentation. Nowadays people think I'm transsexual due to my moniker, Mr. Kate. While I don't have a giant dong between my legs, I'm sure I could bedazzle a mean jockstrap, and I do enjoy sparking people's queries about sexuality and gender, because as my momma always said, "Life is like a box of chocolates—you never know which one's packin' fudge."

#WhyNot **Sometimes you gotta fake wood. Use this easy and clever DIY Faux Bois technique to spruce up an old table and dine with whomever you like.**

DIY Faux Bois

PREP IT

Table (I used a round pedestal dining table from IKEA)

Drop cloth

Latex paint, color of your choice

3-inch-wide paintbrush

Wide-toothed comb

Teasing comb

Plastic fork

Polycrylic sealant, satin finish

DO IT!

1. Set up the table over a drop cloth. (Before you start working on the table itself, you might want to practice this technique on a similar piece of scrap material.) Start by painting a small area of the tabletop in the color of your choice. Note: It's important to only do a small area at a time so the paint is still wet for the faux bois (fake wood) technique.

2. Rake the wide-toothed comb straight over the wet paint area, creating lines where the comb's teeth pick up the paint. Don't worry if it's a little wobbly—it's supposed to look organic, like wood. Wipe off the teeth of the comb on a paper towel or the drop cloth.

3. Use the teasing comb to rake the next row to make a narrow-grained look. This is optional if you'd rather have a wider-grained wood look throughout.

4. Use the plastic fork for the next row and swerve the fork to create one curved area, which will become an "eye" in the wood grain. Using the pointed end of the teasing comb, draw an almond-shaped eye in the paint, inside the curve.

5. Add more paint and repeat the combing and forking technique, varying the position and size of the eyes, until the entire tabletop is covered with a faux bois pattern. Let the paint dry completely.

6. To protect the tabletop from wear and tear, apply a couple of coats of polycrylic sealant on top.

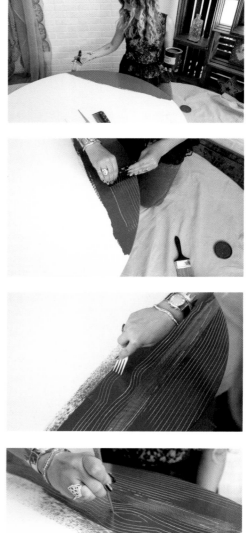

Chapter 35
FAIRY FREAK-OUT

If only love were like the movies.

Love is the most common theme across all films, so naturally our first assignment in film school was to use an old-fashioned Super 8 camera to make a silent movie about . . . love.

Love? I thought, reflecting on my nineteen years on this planet. Well, when I was fourteen, I went to Maui with my parents and had a fling with a Mormon kid from Utah. I was sure I loved him at the time. We set our sights on each other standing in line for the Tarzan rope swing at one of the pools in the tropical resort where we were both staying. He was there with his parents and his five siblings. We'd meet up at night to take "walks" on the beach. He wasn't allowed to drink caffeine, but apparently his religion didn't prohibit him from dry humping in the Jacuzzi.

One night we started making out on the beach. I laid back in the sand—a move that I thought was so sexy—and rolled him over so that I was looming above. I imagined the scenes I'd seen in movies where the girl's hair cascades down as she kisses the handsome man—think *The Little Mermaid*. Instead, my curly hair had picked up a ton of sand and it fell all over his face when I pushed him down. Not what I had planned. Rather than laughing it off, I awkwardly kept kissing him through the gritty sand that now plagued our saliva and his eyeballs. Hardly *South Pacific*.

Thinking about my film, I surmised that that relationship was probably not love, and continued down my rabbit hole of romance.

There was my high school boyfriend, Joaquin Friedman. He was a Puerto Rican Jew who looked like Freddie Prinze Jr. We used to go to his grandma's house for Shabbat and she would make kosher tacos. Gracias.

I dated Joaquin my senior year and then made the mistake of moving with him to Santa Barbara for my freshman year of college, where we lived together in a tiny apartment above our landlord who liked to cook onions and had four loud children. Still reeling from my parents' divorce, I took out my emotions on Joaquin. We fought a lot! One time, in a fit of rage, I hurled a DVD box at him and it hit him near his eye, drawing blood. I felt horrible because I wasn't a violent person, and I realized that Santa Barbara and this relationship weren't for me.

And then there was my current relationship, which was pretty boring. I was dating a fellow film student—this mild-mannered Japanese guy named Han. We mostly hung out in his dorm room, editing slow-motion movies of soccer balls. We were no *Fifty Shades of Grey*. My little sister, Tess, however, was madly in love with Han's little brother Minoru, who lived in Ohio and whom she'd never met.

Han and I had set them up long-distance via the Internet, and they began an adorable thirteen-year-old courtship over the phone.

That's it! I thought to myself. *I'll fly Minoru out here and make their first meeting happen on film!* It sounded like classic, silent movie magic. I started storyboarding as only a pompous teen film student who thinks she knows about love can do.

The plot was this: Tess, a fairy who lives in the woods, one day spots a handsome male tween and falls madly in love with him, as fairies are known to do. She begins stalking this mortal by peering in through the windows of his house. One day he sees her spying on him through his bathroom window while he's undressing to take a shower. He opens the window to shoo her away but she sprinkles fairy dust on him. They share a romantic kiss and go off into the woods to live happily ever after.

Although simple, it was to the point, and more important, it would be fun dressing Tess up as a fairy to meet her true real-life love.

On the day of the film shoot, I dressed Tess in beautiful fairy wings and completed the look with shimmering, fairy-dust-anointed skin. We shot some footage of her climbing trees and peeking in the windows of my dad's house.

As the day progressed, Tess became an increasingly nervous fairy as we waited for Han and Minoru to show up from the airport.

"What if I don't like him in person?" she asked.

"You will!" I assured her. "You guys get along great on the phone."

"Do I have to kiss him when I see him?" she asked, nervously fidgeting with her fairy wings as I checked the film cartridge.

"Tess, you'll be great," I insisted. "He's a nice boy and you're a fairy princess!"

But by the time Han pulled up the long driveway, Tess had spun into a full-on fairy meltdown.

"I can't do it, Kate!" she hissed, as she hid in her closet. "Make them go away!"

"But Tess, he needs to be in the film!" I croaked through the crack in the door. "How am I supposed to replace a fifteen-year-old Japanese love interest at such late notice?"

"*Kate. Make. Them. Leave!*" Tess cried.

I relented. Tess is my kryptonite. I went outside to the car, where Han and his adorable and very nervous-looking brother sat, waiting.

"Hi, guys," I said. "Tess is sick. It's so weird. I think she had an allergic reaction to one of the bushes I made her sit in. So sorry! Can we rain check?"

Minoru looked relieved—Han was annoyed. "He flew all the way out here! How are you going to have your film done by Monday without those scenes?" he asked.

"Oh, I'll figure something out!" I said, desperately reimagining the plot in my head. "Hey, can I borrow some of your clothes, Minoru?" I asked him, eyeballing his suitcase.

"Uh, sure," he said, and retrieved some skater shorts and a baggy T-shirt.

"Can I have a hat, too?" I asked. "Perfect, thank you so much. Have so much fun in LA! Tess says hi!" I shouted as I retreated back into the house.

Inside, I immediately told Tess the new plot: The kiss never happens. Instead, the fairy spies on the boy, but they never actually meet. The fairy is smitten until one day when she sees him driving away with a pretty mortal girl and her heart is broken. She retreats to the trees to live out the rest of her days as a spinster fairy.

"Call Sara and have her come over," I said, referring to Tess's tall best friend. "Tell her she's going to be in a movie."

When Sara showed up, I dressed her in Minoru's clothes, cut up some brown Barbie hair and lash-glued it into her armpit and on her legs, and only shot her from behind. To end the film, I quickly taught thirteen-year-old Sara how to drive my car. She drove it into the sunset while Tess, the forlorn fairy, walked back into the "woods," a.k.a. our neighbor's yard. Tess, relieved that she didn't have to meet her real-life love, was the best fairy I'd ever directed.

#WhyNot **Gold is universally flattering on any skin tone. With the blink of an eye covered in this DIY Gold Fairy-Dust Eye Makeup, make movie magic happen and find yourself in a fairy tale.**

DIY Gold Fairy-Dust Eye Makeup

PREP IT

Eye shadow primer

Translucent face powder and powder brush

Metallic gold eye shadow (I like Make Up For Ever Metal Powder)

Black eyeliner

Black mascara

Lash curler

Eye shadow brush

DO IT!

1. Curl your lashes.

2. Apply eye shadow primer to your lids, pat it in with your fingertip, and set it with translucent face powder.

3. Apply the gold eye shadow all over your lid and along your lower lash line—you could also just stop at the crease of your upper lid, depending on your desired effect.

5. Apply a couple of coats of black mascara on your upper and lower lashes. Wear this look for any occasion!

4. Apply black eyeliner along your upper lash line and lower water line—the inside rim of your lower eyelid.

DO IT Elsewhere! Create a shimmery body butter by mixing gold eye shadow with your favorite lotion!

Chapter 36

TWO BOY-BANDERS AND A BIMBO

My dad was forced to resign from his job as CEO of HBO. He started working there when I was three and was forced out when I was twenty-three. He had been responsible for putting shows like *Sex and the City* and *The Sopranos* on the air, and changed the way we all view cable television. Dad had always taken pride in his work and didn't know what to do with his newfound joblessness. But at least he still had the support of me, my sister, and his bimbo girlfriend.

To try to take his mind off reality, we decided to take a family ski trip at a cozy cabin and spend some quality time together.

Shortly after I started dating Joey, my little sister, Tess, started dating Kyle, the lead singer in Joey's band, The Click Five. That's right, we Albrecht girls were holding down two-fifths of the world's teenage fantasies. The boys had a break from their world tour over the holidays, and we decided to bring our skinny-pant-wearing rockers along for the trip.

My worn-out dad conceded, saying, "Sure. Whatever."

So there we were in Aspen: one depressed fifty-something, two newly-in-love girls, two boy-banders, and a bimbo.

My dad's bimbo girlfriend at the time was north of six feet tall, towering over my dad. Her sense of humor was reminiscent of a twelve-year-old boy and she loved to giggle and wear cleavage-baring tops in the middle of winter. She loved playing games and was energetic and enthusiastic—like an adorable, large-breasted Labrador retriever. Nothing made her laugh harder than a knock-knock joke. I couldn't decide if I wanted to hug her or slap her.

We busied ourselves skiing, cooking dinners, swapping spit with our boyfriends, watching Academy Award screeners, and trying to do the normal things that a functional family would do to try to distract my dad from his melancholic milieu.

One night we were sitting around in a baked ziti coma. Joey and Kyle were doing the dishes and we were all debating which movie to watch. The Bimbo chimed in, "Have you ever played that game 'light as a feather, stiff as a board'?" she asked excitedly, while zipping up a hoodie that was two sizes too small for her boobs.

My dad sighed. "No, baby—what's that?"

"It's a game where you levitate someone with just your fingers and the power of your mind!" she said, trying to sound spooky. A mischievous smile spread across her face.

"It will be so fun!" the Bimbo said, buxomly beaming. "It really works! People really float! You just have to will it."

My dad was grouchy. "It sounds like a silly game," he said. "Let's watch the *There Will Be Blood* screener instead."

The movie sounded like a better option to most of us, and Joey and I really wanted to go make out in the Jacuzzi, but the dejected look on the Bimbo's face swayed us all and we agreed to give it a try.

Excited by our mild willingness, the Bimbo started clearing the dining table. "This will be a perfect place for the person to lie down," she said, gesturing to the tabletop. "Who's going first?"

No one volunteered. There was silence. Finally, my dad stood up from his sunken position on the couch and said, "All right, I'll do it. Let's just do this and get it over with." Obviously he believes in magic. "I have to lay on the table?" he demanded.

"Uh-huh." The Bimbo clapped her manicured hands. My small dad reluctantly heaved himself up on the table and lay down.

The sight of my dad in his pajamas on the dining room table with the Bimbo positioning her hands under his bald head started to seriously tickle our funny bone. Joey, Tess, Kyle, and I were forced to avert our eyes from one another to avoid bursting out laughing and making the Bimbo feel bad.

"Gather around his body," the Bimbo instructed in a hushed, somber tone. *She's really getting into character!* I thought, surprised by her seriousness. She had the sincerity of a cult leader.

Dad crossed his arms over his chest like Count Dracula and each of us placed our first two fingers gently under his body. I was by his leg and Joey was by his torso, with Kyle and Tess on the other side.

"Here lies Chris," the Bimbo began. "We are gathered here today to make him light as a feather and stiff as a board. Let's all say it together."

She nodded for us to join her and we all began chanting in unison, "Light as a feather, stiff as a board," while willing Dad's body to rise completely off the table from the gentle lifting of our awkwardly placed fingers. We were having a bitch of a time trying to conceal our giggles from the busty séance leader. My dad sensed it, too, probably from our quaking hands as we tried to contain ourselves, and a smile started to spread across his face.

Maybe it was one too many servings of the baked ziti, or maybe our dear leader had a bad connection to the dark side, but my dad wasn't budging.

Determined, the Bimbo started yelling, "LIGHT AS A FEATHER, STIFF AS A . . ."

Uh oh—my dad let out a giant snort and that was it, we all crumbled into loud, howling laughter. The Bimbo looked confused, but she grinned anyway.

"'Here lies Chris'!?" my dad exclaimed through his tears of laughter. "I'm not dead!"

The levitation didn't work, but at least we managed to raise his spirits.

#WhyNot **Warm up and float away with this DIY Bleached Feather-Print Scarf.**

DIY Bleached Feather-Print Scarf

PREP IT

A solid, dark-colored silk scarf

Cardboard

Masking tape

Protective gloves

Spray bottle filled with 1 part bleach and 1 part water

A few cruelty-free feathers (see Resources, page 272); you can reuse them if you print in batches

DO IT!

1. In a well-ventilated area, lay a silk scarf flat on a piece of cardboard and tape down the corners with masking tape. Tip: Make your own scarf by hemming a square of silk on all four sides.

2. Wearing gloves, spray the bleach-water mixture liberally on a feather and lightly lay the saturated side down on the silk. This is meant to be an organic pattern, so each feather print will be unique. Tip: The sun helps the bleach to set, so try to do this project outside on a sunny day.

3. Repeat step 2 until you have your desired feather print.

4. Wait until the feathers and scarf are dry before removing the feathers, and then wear your scarf or frame it as art!

DO IT Elsewhere! Use feathers covered in porcelain paint to create decorative feather print plates! Bake them in a low-temperature oven to cure the paint and style them on your walls or use as a jewelry holder.

Chapter 37
SLOPPY SASHIMI

"I haven't smoked pot since my twenties!" my mom exclaimed to me. "Can I have some?"

I was aghast! My mom was asking her seventeen-year-old daughter for pot! All of a sudden, marijuana seemed *waaaay* less cool.

"I used to smoke in my tiny apartment in New York and clean it from top to bottom," she recalled. "I'd love to have some if you can get it for me."

Her divorce had turned my mom into a desperate teenager.

I agreed, and let her smoke with my friends, thinking I'd be known for having a "cool mom." My friends thought it was hilarious, but as she was having a giggling fit with my friends after spilling pickle juice on my bed, I quickly realized that it was the worst decision ever.

"Go clean the house," I told her as I coaxed the bloodshot-eyed zombie mom out of my room with a pint of Ben & Jerry's and locked the door behind her.

Drugs never became my thing. I like being in control—plus, my parents did enough drugs for two generations. I love a nice glass of wine or a martini to get loose with friends, a.k.a. watching reality TV by myself on the couch, but these days that's the extent of my brain cell killing.

The last time I did drugs, it was by accident.

My sister, Tess, was in town visiting from New York, and we were going to celebrate with a nice sister dinner at a swanky sushi restaurant. Stressed from writing this fucking book, I had a bad headache. On my way out the door, I grabbed the Tylenol out of the medicine cabinet and took three of them . . . one more than my usual two tablets, but I wanted to feel my best for the night ahead.

I was wearing my new white baby-doll dress and had spent the extra thirty minutes it takes to blow-dry my mop of a head. I hopped in my car and drove across town to meet Tess.

The restaurant was fabulous and super crowded. Jessica Alba (love her) was two tables away from us, and I was so glad we had made a reservation and got seated right away. Halfway through my first tiny glass of sake, I felt really drunk.

"This sake is so strong!" I slurred. "Are you feeling it?"

My sister shook her head, then caught my elbow as it drifted off the table.

"What's wrong with you?" she hissed. "You're a mess!"

I started to freak out. My limbs were feeling like floppy pieces of sashimi, and I could barely raise my hand.

"Oh, shit," I said in slow motion. "Somebody roofied me!" I yelled.

Tess hushed me, turning to our neighbors and laughing nervously. "She's kidding," she assured them, then turned back to me. "You didn't get roofied, you freak. We're drinking from the same bottle of sake!"

I started crying sloppily.

"Did you drink before dinner?" Tess asked, annoyed.

Suddenly it dawned on me. The clouds in my head parted and for a fleeting moment I remembered that when I grabbed the Tylenol out of the bottle, in my rush out the door, I thought they looked a little smaller than usual.

"Ohhh shittt!" I slurred. "Tess! Fuuuck! I think I took three muzzle relazers!"

Months earlier I had visited my mom in New York and had thrown out my neck sleeping on the Murphy bed. My mom, always with a veritable pharmacy in her purse, told me to take a muscle relaxer and gave me four extra for later, which I stored in an empty Tylenol bottle, to be forgotten . . . until now.

"What!" Tess exclaimed, pulling me back to the reality that was getting fuzzier by the second. "Why?"

My head slumped forward, dunking my hair into my soy sauce. Tess palmed my forehead, supporting the weight of my head. My blow-dried hair dripped soy sauce down my white dress.

"Ugh, Kate! I gotta get you outta here." Tess got our check. I told the waitress she had a "fabulous blousssssssss."

Tess hoisted me toward the exit of the restaurant, carrying me against her five-foot-two frame.

On our way out, I recognized a casting director whom I had auditioned for in the past. I nodded her way, smiled, and a little drool came out of my mouth. She looked away in embarrassed horror, probably thinking, *How sad, another failed actress is going downhill at a young age!*

"Tessss, can we get isss cream on the way home?" I slurped, sucking my drool back in my mouth as she pushed me out of the restaurant.

#WhyNot **Getting cracked out and losing your marbles isn't cute, but this DIY Cracked-Marble Tray is.**

DIY Cracked-Marble Tray

PREP IT

A tray with a deeper rim than the depth of a flat-back marble

Flat-back marbles, enough to fill your tray

Baking sheet

Protective eyewear and oven mitts

Bowl of ice water

Epoxy resin—1 or 2 boxes, depending on the size of your tray

Disposable container to mix the resin

Popsicle sticks or some other disposable stirrer

DO IT!

1. Preheat the oven to 500°F and lay the marbles on the baking sheet.

2. Heat the marbles for 20 minutes. Put on protective eyewear and oven mitts, then dump the hot marbles in a bowl of ice water, which will get them to crack. (The eyewear is important in case a rogue marble cracks violently—it's never happened to me, but don't risk it.)

3. Spread the cracked marbles on a towel to dry, then arrange them in the tray.

4. Follow the instructions on the box of epoxy resin—usually they say to heat up the two bottles of epoxy ingredients in warm water and stir equal parts together in a disposable container for around 4 minutes. Stir the resin slowly with the Popsicle stick to avoid air bubbles.

5. Slowly pour the resin mixture over your tray of marbles, covering them completely to create a flat surface. You may need to stir up another batch of resin to fully fill the tray base and cover all the marbles. Tip: Use the Popsicle stick to gently pop any stubborn bubbles to leave a smooth finish.

6. Let the resin cure for 72 hours in a still, dust-free area. Style the tray in your interior space!

DO IT Elsewhere! Glue earring posts to the flat backs of two cracked marbles to make a pair of stud earrings!

Chapter 38
HOUSE PROM

Prom was upon us. At my tiny high school, with only eighty kids, the prom was an event that the entire school attended. The dance always had a theme. Not lacking creativity or weirdness, my hippie school's prom themes ranged from Mountain Gnome Paradise to Pilgrims and Pirates. The senior class was always responsible for planning and booking the event, and this year I was a senior. Because we were few and the budget was small, the dance usually took place at some weird restaurant or, in this particular case, at my friend Tom's house.

Our senior class held a meeting to plan the (little) big event. Various ideas were shouted out for a location:

"Mini golf!"

"Magic Mountain!"

"Downtown LA!"

"My house!"

So we settled on . . . Tom's house. Our reasoning was that if we didn't have to spend money on a venue, we could blow it out with our decorating and food spread. Plus, Tom's dad did voiceovers for movie trailers, and they lived in a big house in the Valley with a large garage that could serve as our ballroom, and their live-in housekeeper was famous for her fajitas.

We decided on a Heaven and Hell theme. A classic.

I knew I had to be elected prom decorator. The prom would be the largest-scale decorating project I'd ever attempted, my only previous projects being my bedrooms, motel rooms, and my camp dorm room when I was twelve. I spent the night creating a mood board with my vision for the event and presented it to the class with pomp and grandeur. I was awarded the position. No one else wanted it.

My design scheme included a food and drink table made to resemble Hell, with a red tablecloth, lava rocks, and black candles. The dance floor would be Heaven, with suspended clouds, and the outside patio would feature heavenly twinkle lights and tinsel.

My mom and I headed to the giant craft emporium in downtown LA to buy all the supplies: reams of tissue paper for the lava rocks, bags and bags of white pillow stuffing for the clouds, twinkle lights, tinsel, and even a basket full of fake pearls to create the pearly gates photo backdrop. This was going to be the most magnificent prom ever!

The problem was my team. My senior classmates were a less-than-motivated bunch, and when I showed up at Tom's house the morning of prom, they had all gone to see a movie. I was left there, alone, with my bags of supplies and the family's stinky dog, Fatty. Infuriated by their teenage ineptitude and overwhelmed by the task at hand, I called upon my knight with shining ladder, Manuel, our gardener/handyman.

By the time my classmates returned from the movie, they found me, Manuel, and Frida the fajita master putting the finishing touches on what I didn't want to admit was just an okay-looking house prom. The lava rocks looked more like trash, the clouds had a less-than-heavenly sag, and we'd blown out a few strands of the twinkle lights. Not the masterpiece I had imagined, but still pretty darn good-looking for a garage.

With the dance starting in a couple of hours, I hurried home to get dressed. I had purchased my Hell-inspired ensemble at a vampire store on Hollywood Boulevard. The good thing about living in LA is that there's a store for every persuasion. The store, Death Becomes Her, was decked out with corsets and full-length velvet gowns for women and ruffly shirts and coats for men. I had picked out a long dress that had a full midnight blue satin skirt topped off by a black velvet bodice with an embroidered pentagram. My boobs were struggling to fill the ample cups of the bodice, so I put a sock under each breast to give them that plumpy vampiress look. I used super-strength hair gel to style two devil horns in my short hair and dyed the tips red with food coloring. I had my boyfriend, Joaquin, wear a tuxedo with tails so we looked cohesive.

On the short limousine ride from my neighborhood to Tom's, my excitement mounted in anticipation of what was sure to be the most perfect prom ever.

Walking up to the house, I saw Tom approaching with a grim look on his face.

"The dog ate Hell," he said, flatly.

"What do you mean!?" I exclaimed.

"Fatty chewed up all your tissue paper lava and peed on the Pearly Gates." He looked apologetic, acknowledged Joaquin with a nod, and sauntered off.

Joaquin calmed me down and we went inside. Hell's inferno was soggy balls of orange tissue remnants, and one of my idiot classmates was wearing Heaven's cloud on his head. I tried to enjoy myself. We posed for photos, danced, and did the usual prom activities. I was further dismayed when the other half of my twinkle light strands burned out, leaving a black hole in what was supposed to be a heavenly patio.

Tom's parents and little sisters kept coming in and checking on us, none of them dressed on theme, and the little girls were even in pajamas. It was dreadful. Don't ever have your prom at home.

> #WhyNot **Bring a little piece of the heavens into your home with these DIY Constellation Lanterns.**

DIY Constellation Lanterns

PREP IT

Paper lantern(s)

Chalkboard paint

Small to medium paintbrush

Large embroidery needle

Light cord kit and lightbulb

White chalk

Small to medium screw hook and appropriate anchor

DO IT!

1. Unfold the lantern and use the inner wire bracket to secure it.

2. Gently paint the lantern with chalkboard paint and let dry. You may need two coats of paint.

3. Poke holes in the paper lantern with the needle. Wiggle the needle around a bit once inserted to make the holes large enough for the light to peek through as your shining stars.

4. Season the chalkboard paint by rubbing it with chalk first and gently wiping it off. Use chalk to gently draw constellations on the lantern.

5. Insert the light cord kit and lightbulb inside the lantern. Use the screw hook and anchor to hang the lantern from the ceiling near a plug, or run an extension cord outside and hang the lantern from a tree branch.

DO IT Elsewhere! Paint your nails black and use white nail polish and a toothpick to create the dots and lines for constellation nail art!

Chapter 39
MY MOM THE MANATEE

"Don't worry, I didn't get beat up," my mom said as I stared, aghast, at her swollen, bruised face. "I paid for this!"

I'm not sure that when the pioneers crossed the treacherous Sierra Nevada mountains to settle in California, they would have predicted that their descendants would risk their lives to put large hills on their chests. Modern-day Angelenos treat a trip to the plastic surgeon like a trip to Starbucks. "Do I go for a grande or venti penile implant?" one might ask oneself . . . on a Thursday.

There was a time when I was in high school that my mom checked out of life and checked in—to hospitals. She was there to get "tune-ups" and would come home with various bruises and bandages or, worse, drainage bags—clear plastic sacks attached to tubes that were embedded in her flesh to catch the fluid released from all the swelling. This was totally normal. I'd come home from school, pour myself a glass of Hibiscus Cooler, and tell my mom about my day, trying to avoid eye contact with her fluid bag, the contents of which resembled my refreshing beverage to an alarming degree.

Mom was always really open about her procedures. She was known to publicly lift her shirt at the horse show competitions we attended to show the gay horse trainers her newly "lifted tits." She passed out her doctor's info to anyone who showed a mild interest, and it wasn't long before everyone was walking around with their very own fluid bags and maxi pads taped to their tummies to act as giant Band-Aids.

I didn't really mind my mom getting plastic surgery. She seemed pretty nonchalant about it and never ended up looking too scary after things healed. I got used to her looking as if she'd gotten hit by a truck, but the thing I hated was the pain pills.

Her doctor would prescribe her gnarly drugs that turned her into a loopy, swollen, bruised, moaning mermaid . . . not the beautiful water nymphs of myths, but the manatee kind—a sea cow. My mom would flop around on her bed, making guttural noises with her flesh, the bloated purple color of a blubberous sea mammal. Her words seamed together, and she'd often drool.

"Kate, couchuu bring me some tatershipss," she'd slur, and I'd fetch her kettle chips on my way to do my homework.

Hired private nurses attended to her after she returned home from her trips to the doctor. They were usually nice, portly Jamaican ladies who slept on the couch and woke up periodically to give her more drugs and keep my mom a happy manatee. On one post-surgery occasion, I was talking to my mom in the kitchen, right after she had taken a Percocet and was eating some salad—manatees are vegetarians. She was leaning on her hand with her elbow propped on the kitchen counter and the fork, with a lonely piece of lettuce, was very close to her eye. I watched as the Percocet took over, her sentence lilting off and her glassy eyes rolling in her head. Her head started to droop toward the fork spikes inches away, and I yelled "Mom!" just in time to jerk her back to semi-reality and not poke her eye out. Not sure how Doctor Plastic would have fixed fork-in-eye syndrome.

In her painkiller haze, Mom would often make rash decisions, like the time she decided to go back to the doctor after she had gotten a facelift to have him also give her breast implants. She came home with drains coming out of her head and chest and couldn't lift her arms or turn her head. She did, however, decide she wanted to start a journaling group.

"Fajah tolll me she hasa connecshun to get beuutiful Indian fabricsss," my mom told me, looking like an excited mummy in her head bandages and feebly gesturing to Fajah, her hired nurse. "I wanna buy sssome and make long flowwy kimonos for our girlfriendss and we can wearr them and journal when it's the full moonss."

I nodded. "Sure," I said. "Makes total sense."

The next day Fajah showed up with $3,000 worth of gorgeous, intricately embroidered Indian fabrics from her "connection." Fajah displayed each one in front of my mom's face, since she couldn't turn her head to look at the pile.

My mom never made the fabrics into kimonos, nor did we ever journal with girlfriends under the full moon. The fabrics stayed in a neat pile in the top shelf of her closet until I moved into my first apartment in Santa Barbara during my freshman year of college.

"Let's use my beautiful Indian fabrics to upholster the walls and ceiling in your apartment!" Mom exclaimed. With no surgical procedures currently on her calendar, my move to college would be her new operation.

"Sure," I said. "Makes total sense."

And we did just that. We broke out the electric staple gun and the gorgeous embroidered fabrics, and my mom lifted her arms and got to work.

#WhyNot **Avoid the bloating, bruises, and price tag of surgery and highlight your natural beauty with glamorous DIY Easy Makeup Contouring.**

DIY Easy Makeup Contouring

PREP IT

Foundation, a few shades lighter than your skin tone (I like using liquid for more natural-looking coverage)

Foundation, a few shades darker than your skin tone

Foundation, in your skin tone

Foundation brush

Stipple brush or blending sponge

Blush

DO IT!

1. Apply the light foundation to the center of your forehead, under your eyebrow, on the bridge of your nose, on the tops of your cheekbones, above your upper lip, on the tip of your chin, and along the top of your jawline.

2. Apply dark foundation to your temples, either side of your nose, the indent of your cheeks, the base of your jawline, the sides of your neck, and just beneath your collarbone.

3. Combine the dark and light shades by dipping the stipple brush in a little bit of your tone foundation and blending it all together using circular motions.

4. Finish with a little blush on the apples of your cheeks.

Chapter 40
POOP IN THE BATHTUB

I used to refer to the guys I'd set my romantic sights on as "projects." Guys that presented a challenge always enticed me, and I especially liked smart, weird, or adorably innocent dudes who I could bring to the dark side.

I was twenty-one, in college, and studying film production. My project for the semester was Henry, whose smoldering brown eyes and passion for space operas made him a dork and completely oblivious to my mounting attraction. He was a mean dork, a breed of dork prominent around film school, the kind that will defend his dorky honor to the death. "Yes, abso-fuckin-lutely *Starfighter* is better than *The Wrath of Khan!*"

I would try my darndest to get some one-on-one time with Henry and suggest things in class like, "Can we go off in teams of two for this discussion on sexual tension in film noir?" as I'd slyly look at Henry, who seemed more interested in the weird stain on his corduroys than my sexual advances.

One day in Spaghetti Westerns 101, Henry made an announcement inviting the class to Little Tokyo to watch his friend's band perform. I thought, *This is my chance! A social outing with copious amounts of alcohol and my best Klingon cleavage will definitely lure him into my clutches!*

The band sucked—it was one of the screaming varieties that put a sourpuss on the old Japanese man who owned the dive bar—but it ignited an uncharacteristically gleeful Headbanging Henry. To numb my eardrums and my nerves, I sucked down five too many Long Island iced teas. I guess the fact that I was the only other person in the bar headbanging to his friend's band's crappy music was the straw that broke the camel's camera lens, and I ended up going home with Henry to "sleep it off."

We slept in his twin bed in the room he shared with his equally dorky and mean roommate. Henry was a decent kisser, but staring at a poster of Chewbacca while Henry tried to locate my R2-G-Spot was soberingly earthbound.

I woke at around six in the morning with an excruciating headache and only one thought running through my head: *I have to poop!*

I went into Henry's dirty bathroom and proceeded to have a very hungover poo. Apparently, too many Long Island iced teas make you pee out of your butt.

Even though I was in agony, I maintained my ladylike manners and tried to do a courtesy flush to keep the smell from permeating into the bedroom beyond. Wouldn't you know, the toilet *wouldn't flush!?* My panic acted as a butt plug. I still had to go, but I knew I *had* to get that toilet to flush, because otherwise this "project" that I had worked too hard to snare would be confronted by the B-movie horror scene in his toilet. I flushed again and prayed to the gods of one-night stands. The damn thing just filled with more water, threatening to spill over the sides. Oh no, this was quickly becoming like a scene from *Waterworld*. I grabbed the red Solo cup where Henry and his roomie stored their toothbrushes and used it to scoop some excess water out of the toilet and into the plastic trash can. I piled toilet paper in the trash can and into the toilet to mask the liquid contents. The scene was not cute, but it could pass for a "I just went pee and your toilet didn't flush!" situation. But *ooohhh shit!*—I still had to *go!*

There was only one bathroom in Henry's dumpy love lair, and the area of LA he lived in had no close-by restaurant or shops—plus, it was 6:15 A.M. on Saturday! I knew I had to get this Long Island poison out of my body, so I did what any self-respecting, hungover twenty-one-year-old would do: I pooped in the tub.

It made total sense to me in the moment. My poo was liquid, and the tub drain was more trustworthy than the toilet, so I sat on the edge of his tub and reenacted *Psycho*.

After I was done I thoroughly rinsed out the tub using his Selsun Blue, disposed of my wiping tissues in the trash can, and wet my hair in the sink to justify the tub being wet, because duh, I wasn't actually going to take a real shower in my emergency toilet! I gotta draw the line somewhere.

I crawled back into Henry's bed, headache still thumping but tummy nice and empty. Later in the morning I acted surprised when I saw the toilet. "God, boys are so gross."

Henry drove me to my car in his pickup truck while we listened to the soundtrack from *I Know What You Did Last Summer*.

#WhyNot **Don't find yourself in a poopy situation. Cover your tracks with this aromatherapy DIY Pre-Poo Spray.**

DIY Pre-Poo Spray

PREP IT

Little funnel

20 drops lemongrass essential oil

9 drops geranium essential oil

3 drops tangerine essential oil

6 drops lavender essential oil

Perfume or spray bottle

Purified water

DO IT

1. Funnel all the drops of oil into the spray bottle and fill it with water.

2. To use: Shake the bottle and spray a few pumps over the unused surface of the toilet water to keep your doody fumes from tainting the room!

DO IT Elsewhere! Make your spray bottle look glamorous with a vintage reproduction pump atomizer you can purchase online or at the flea market!

Chapter 41

MY GRANDMA THE BITCH

My grandma is a bitch—the kind of bitch you want on your side. The kind that will shake her tiny fist at anyone who crosses her granddaughters.

She is a native New "Yawker." She loves Chris Rock—like, dies laughing whenever she watches his stand-up shows—and has been known to cuss out bike riders who use the sidewalk instead of the bike lane. "These fucking bikes are taking over the city!" she yells, standing in her miniature Manhattan kitchen and brandishing her tomato-sauce-covered wooden spoon (she's half Italian and a great cook).

When I was little, Granny would visit LA and take me to the park. One time, I was playing on the swings with the other kids and all of a sudden there was yelling. I looked up to see little Granny pointing at the

Don't mess with my Grandma. She'll throw rocks at you.

bushes on the far side of the playground where a man was creepily tucked behind the foliage.

"I see you, you creep!" she yelled, pointing her bony finger at him.

The other mothers looked aghast and the creep looked startled.

"You get away from these kids! What are you, a pervert? This is a playground, not a place for old men!" She started toward him.

With all eyes on the creep, he stepped out of the bushes and opened his mouth to protest, but Granny cut him off before he got a word out.

"Don't you utter a word, you sicko!" Granny screamed and picked up a plastic shovel out of the sandbox. The shovel was attached to a plastic bucket, but she nevertheless brandished the whole weird assortment of sand toys at him menacingly as she advanced in his direction.

"I'm not going to say it again—*get outta heeea.*" She sounded like a really shrill Fonzie.

The guy looked genuinely freaked, grabbed a bag of gardening tools, ran to his pickup truck, and took off. Granny had just chased off the gardener.

One hot, sticky New York summer I stayed with Granny and Grandpa at their apartment in the Bronx. They lived near the projects, where it was customary to crack open a fire hydrant on a hot day so the kids could play in the spraying water. Granny wanted me to experience these urban rapids, so she marched me up to a large group of children who were much older than five-year-old me and instructed them to step aside so her granddaughter could get sprayed. She threatened to seal the hydrant if they didn't move. They heeded her request, and all eyes were on me as I got an exclusive tummy pummeling by the exploding nozzle. It was delightful.

Once when my sister was in daycare, a three-year-old boy threw sand in her eyes. Tess told Granny, and the hit was out. The next day when Granny dropped off Tess, she sidled up to the boy, out of earshot of the daycare teachers, and whispered, "I'm a real-life witch, and if you throw sand at Tessie again, I'm going to turn you into a frog!" The petrified toddler was on his best behavior from that point on, and thankfully Granny was never arrested for harassment.

These days Joey and I often stay at Granny's apartment when we visit New York City. We always try to bring her a thank-you gift for hosting us, and so far she's given back to us all but one of them—a cane with a decorative handle, which she decided would be the perfect weapon to jam into the spokes of bicyclists as they passed her "illegally" on the sidewalk.

Over Granny's dining room table hangs her spirit animal: a portrait of the Grinch Who Stole Christmas that my sister painted for her, to remind anyone who dines at her table that she is a proud curmudgeon.

When my grandfather was dying of lung cancer, Granny was his constant caretaker. She'd make him her famous chicken noodle soup to soothe his searing throat, and change his pajamas every day. She was incessantly caring. One day she was making him roll over to avoid getting bedsores from his hospice bed, and he turned to her with a smile on his face and said, "You're such a pushy bitch!"

She loves that story. She tells it often. She's such a bitch.

#WhyNot **Take your grandma's doilies and tell them to kiss your butt with this DIY Granny Chic Doily Skirt.**

DIY Granny Chic Doily Skirt

PREP IT

Skirt

Thirty 6-inch doilies, more or less depending on the size of your skirt

Pins

Hot glue gun and clear fabric hot glue sticks

DO IT!

1. Put on the skirt and pin the doilies on in rows, starting from the bottom hem up toward your waist. You want to wear your skirt when pinning to ensure that the doilies are glued to fit the skirt as it's worn, but be careful not to stick yourself with the pins—get a friend or your grandma to help you!

2. Carefully remove the skirt and hot-glue the doilies in place exactly where you pinned them, starting with the top row, but glue only at the top and sides of your doilies. Leave the center and bottoms free and clear to allow for stretching around your lovely curves!

DO IT Elsewhere! Paint a canvas black and glue doilies in a cascading arrangement for an edgy girly art piece.

Chapter 42

BILLIONAIRE BUST

My best friend is a billionaire. There are so many other things about him that really define who he is: a funny, kind, intelligent, loyal, and very talented guy. But the fact remains that he grew up as a billionaire . . . which for a kid, is super weird.

I met Nathaniel at the horse shows, where we competed in the same equestrian jumping division. His nannies would cheer him on from the stands while his parents vacationed in the Caribbean. I was sixteen and he was an awkward, chubby twelve-year-old with a killer sense of humor. We were an odd pair, but we got along great. He even invited me to his bar mitzvah at his Beverly Hills compound.

Nathaniel had the most bizarre upbringing out of any of my friends. He lived in a gargantuan Beverly Hills mansion with a staff of twenty. Sleepovers at Nathaniel's house were the weirdest and most indulgent I have ever experienced. I'd sleep in one of the exquisitely decorated guestrooms, where one of the seven white-uniformed maids had already turned down the bed for me. It was better than any service you'd experience in even the nicest five-star hotels. The maids would peel back the luxurious bedding just so and leave a glass pitcher of water and a bowl of fresh fruit on the beautiful chest of drawers next to the sumptuous bed . . . you know, in case you wanted to nibble on some strawberries in the middle of the night. This was life as usual for Nathaniel.

My favorite sleepover amenity was the pets. We had the option to phone down to the guard house to bring us up a dog or three to cuddle with at night. Nathaniel's mom broke the only-three-dogs-allowed-per-household-in-Beverly-Hills rule by twelve! They had fifteen dogs on the property, complete with their own full-time staff. At night the dogs were kept in kennels near the East Guard Gate—yes, that means there was also a West Guard Gate—so that all we had to do was buzz down to the security guards via the intercom system that webbed through the entire house and say, "Can you please send up Duchess and Duke and, hmmm, maybe Chiquita as well to Nathaniel's room? Thank you!"

Moments later, in would walk two adorable poodles and one Chihuahua carried by a giant uniformed security guard . . . much better than stuffed animals.

Being older than Nathaniel meant that I was more experienced and could expose him to the normal world outside his gates. He smoked his first cigarette with me in my car while we were parked in front of the mansion but far enough away to be out of the reach of the cameras. I felt guilty that I was being a bad influence, but he wanted a partner in crime, and I was available.

The first time we smoked pot together, he had begged me to try to get some, so I called our high school "drug dealer." His name was Mitch and his dad was the glass-blowing teacher at my school. He was the bad boy with his lowered Honda Civic and could always score whatever you needed from his public school connections. Mitch came over to my house and we ceremoniously smoked Nathaniel out for his first time. He got so high that he was rolling around on the floor talking to my two Siamese cats in Hebrew. Mitch took him for a drive to calm him down, but he was just having a blast the entire time, his contagious laugh erupting out of his chubby body every time he opened his mouth.

Nathaniel decided he loved the whole thing so much that he bought a giant bag of Mitch's stickiest Mendocino County weed, which Nathaniel hid under his socks in the bottom drawer of his semiprecious inlay dresser.

A couple of days later, one of the seven maids found the giant stash of marijuana under his socks. . . . You could never keep anything from housekeeping! The maid gave it to the nanny, who then turned it over to Nathaniel's parents. Over the intercom, Nathaniel's dad summoned him to his study. The nanny marched Nathaniel the half mile down the hallway and two staircases to the giant library that was his dad's home office. Nathaniel's dad had his pet monkey perched on his shoulder and the bag of weed on his leather desk. Nathaniel promptly blamed the whole thing on me . . . after all, what are older friends for?

Nathaniel is now an entertainment lawyer and holds a medical marijuana card for his I-live-in-an-apartment-with-no-nanny-or-turn-down-service "anxiety."

#WhyNot **Make your room look like a billion bucks with a DIY Malachite Dresser in which to keep your precious things.**

DIY Malachite Dresser

PREP IT

Wood dresser

Tissue paper in 3 different shades of green—I used light mint, kelly green, and dark green

Decoupage glue, like Mod Podge

Foam brush

Paper plate

Cup of water

DO IT!

1. Remove the dresser drawers. Use a foam brush to paint your entire dresser and drawers with the decoupage glue—you may want to work on one small area at a time. Lay down a sheet of the lightest shade of green tissue paper and gently paint over the sheet with another layer of glue. Work with smaller pieces of paper to avoid air bubbles and use a little water mixed with the glue to help make the paper more flexible.

2. Rip strips of the two darker shades of paper and decoupage those over the lighter layer, leaving some light green exposed. Make sure you apply decoupage glue to the area before and after you lay down each strip. It's best to go from lightest to darkest when applying the tissue paper, so the darkest shade of green should be the last layer applied. Tip: Malachite doesn't have to be just stripes—get a different look by layering ripped circular shapes.

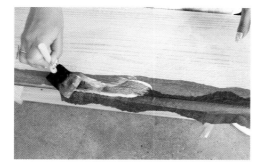 

3. Repeat step 2 until your entire dresser is covered.

4. Seal your dresser with multiple coats of decoupage glue, letting each one dry before applying the next. You can get an even stronger seal using a finishing coat of clear polyacrylic, applied with a paintbrush.

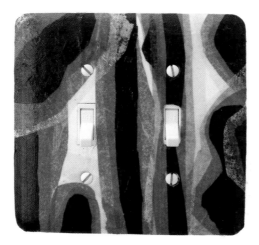

DO IT Elsewhere! Fancy up your light switch with the same decoupage malachite technique!

Chapter 43
KILLING GHOSTS WITH BLOW-DRYERS

I attempted to murder a ghost when I was seventeen. It was the year my parents had gotten divorced, and with the pretense that all was amicable, my dad moved into a house a couple of blocks away from our family home in the same gated community. Their plan was to stay friendly and co-parent. Boy, were they wrong! My dad immediately struck up a relationship with his horse-trainer girlfriend, and my mom, sister, and I were expected to just accept and be cool with it after my parents' twenty-year marriage.

I rarely slept over at my dad's new house because I didn't like that he had moved on so quickly. My sister, Tess, and I also had to deal with the horse trainer gf moving in, along with her two young kids. I was old enough to say, "Fuck you, I'm going to smoke cigarettes," but my ten-year-old sister was forced to become an insta-sibling to a seven-year-old girl and a four-year-old boy. On the occasions that I did stay over, I made sure it was when the horse trainer wasn't there, and I was usually accompanied by my boyfriend at the time, Joaquin. My dad didn't like that my college freshman boyfriend was spending the night, but he didn't have much leverage since he was acting like a lusty teen himself. I stayed there only to stay close to my split-custody-suffering little sister.

The house had all kinds of weird vibes, which I attributed to the taint of my dad's new relationship, but it turns out it was actually haunted.

One night my dad was out for the evening doing something show business-y, and Joaquin, Tess, and I were cozy on my bed, watching a movie and munching on a pineapple pizza. All was momentarily, blissfully okay, with the crazy adults and surrogate siblings out of the house, until suddenly, out of my peripheral vision, I saw something pass across the open doorway and—dare I say it—float toward the descending staircase! I nearly choked on a piece of cheese-covered pineapple. The figure was the size of an average human, all white and kind of featureless, but what struck an eerie fear in me was its posture—it looked sad, defeated. I jumped to scream but my reasonable brain kicked in, immediately convincing myself I had imagined everything. At the same instant I reasoned the vision away, my sister pointed at the doorway and said, "I just saw something walk past that door!"

I'm sure my face turned as white as, well, a ghost, but I didn't want to scare Tess. I quietly asked, "What did you see?"

She described the same exact thing that I had seen. "It looked like a person, with a hood or something, and it was white and it floated! I'm scared."

I panicked. I was scared, too—we had both seen something that was, by some definition, real.

"Oh my God," I said, looking at Joaquin, as I jumped up to close the door to my room. "I totally saw it, too—there's something in the house! What do we do!?"

Joaquin thought we were crazy.

"You guys didn't see anything!" he said. "You're probably just scared from the movie."

"Joaquin," I said sternly, "we're watching *Trading Places*. It's not a scary movie. We need to get this thing out of the house!"

Not being well versed in ghost busting, I wasn't sure what to do. We couldn't call the police; I didn't think LAPD would respond to ghost sightings. I thought about calling the private security that manned the guard gates of the gated community for back-up, but that seemed like a long shot. Bottom line was that my dad needed to get his ass back to the house to help us fight off this sad spirit. *You got divorced, a new girlfriend with kids, and now a ghost!?* I admonished him in my mind. This was too much!

I called my dad from the phone in my room and told him he needed to come home ASAP. He told me I was overreacting.

"Tess and I both saw the same exact thing!" I said. "Now we're locked in my room. You have to come kill it and rescue us!"

My dad seized the moment to emasculate Joaquin. "Why doesn't Joaquin go look for the ghost? He's a strong guy."

"Dad!" I yelled. "We don't have any weapons! I'm not sending him out there unarmed."

I hung up, disgusted that my dad wasn't recognizing the gravity of the situation. I felt like I really couldn't count on him for anything these days.

Joaquin had taken the bait. "I can go out there," he said, now looking a little scared.

I didn't want to send him out to the void of a haunted house alone, so I got to hunting for weapons for all three of us inside my room and the connecting bathroom. The heaviest things I could find were my alarm clock, a blow-dryer, and a platform shoe. I gave Joaquin the clock, I took the blow-dryer, and I gave tiny Tess the giant, neon-swirled platform go-go boot. Lining up with Joaquin in front, Tess in the middle, and me in the back, we quietly opened the bedroom door and tiptoed out to the landing.

"I saw it walk, err, float, toward the stairs," I hissed.

"Me too," whispered Tess, her brown eyes looking extra big.

We inched our frightened conga line toward the stairs, each of us brandishing our weapons. We crept down the stairs and through the entire bottom floor of the house, opening each closet door and yelling a collective "raaawr" every time a door swung open, hoping to scare the thing before it could scare us. We were as ill equipped to handle ghosts as we were divorce.

My dad came home to find the three of us outside in the Jacuzzi—the only place we felt safe. We made him comb the house thoroughly, and when his efforts turned up nothing, I told him he needed to hire a professional exorcist. He didn't.

"Just say, 'This isn't your home anymore, please go away,'" he instructed.

That seemed too passive to me in my post-traumatic state, although I did wish I could say those exact words to his girlfriend.

My aversion to that house was now solidified. From that day on, I wouldn't be there alone. I told that ghost so many times, "Please go away, you're not welcome here, I don't like this house at all, so I'm sure there are better places for you. If you do choose to stay, please don't appear to me or Tess anymore, but you're welcome to scare the shit out of the horse trainer girlfriend."

When Dad eventually moved out of that house, he told us that the real estate broker had informed him that the prior owners had been murdered by their children for insurance money.

Must have been a shitty divorce.

#WhyNot **Ghosts and time have one thing in common: They don't die. Kill time with this fun DIY Fighting Time Wall Clock.**

DIY Fighting Time
Wall Clock

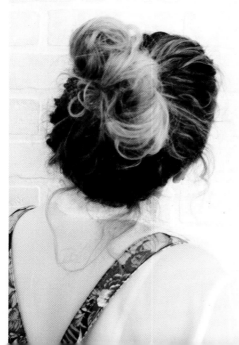

PREP IT

Spray paint for the soldiers

12 toy soldiers

Drop cloth

Masking tape

Battery-operated clock movement

Paint to match your wall color

Paint for the clock hands (optional)

Paint-safe wall mounting, like Command Small Picture Hanging Strips

DO IT!

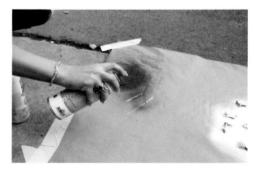

2. Use masking tape to protect the battery area and threaded shaft of the clock movement, then paint the body of the clock movement to match the wall color. Paint the hands of the clock a contrasting color. Let dry, then twist on the clock hands.

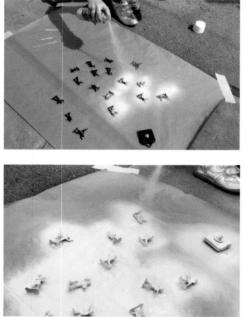

1. Spray-paint the toy soldiers outside on a drop cloth or scrap cardboard. Let dry and paint the other side. Tip: If you want to paint the soldiers a lighter color, prime them first with white primer or spray paint.

3. Mount the clock movement and toy soldiers in a surrounding circle directly to the wall using pieces of the wall mounting strips (you may need to cut the strips smaller to fit under the base of the toy soldiers).

DO IT Elsewhere! Painted toy soldiers holding tiny paper flowers are fierce and fabulous decorations or place card holders.

Chapter 44

CLEANSING BACHELORETTES

I hate Vegas. I don't like air-conditioning, fake Paris, strippers, or sad people losing all their money.

I was set to be a bridesmaid in the wedding of my dear friend Bea, who was having her bachelorette party in the aforementioned city of too many all-you-can-eat buffets. I had met Bea several years earlier when we were acting in a movie together, and we became great friends. Bea had moved to LA after attending college in Florida and had been in a sorority. The bachelorette party was going to be a mix of her Florida sorority sisters and her snarky LA friends.

The sorority sister friend in charge of organizing the trip emailed everyone saying there would be four girls per room. The LA girls would room together and the Florida girls would room together, but because of the numbers, two Florida girls would be paired up with two LA girls. The LA girls quickly paired up with each other, and I got put with Samantha, a self-proclaimed yenta who does voiceovers for cartoons, along with two sorority strangers. I always got along great with Samantha in LA but had never shared a bed with her. Samantha liked to complain, usually about her weight, the temperature, other people, or whatever diet she was on that "wasn't working." I assumed Samantha would insist on sleeping with only a top sheet and immediately hate our roommates—our room would be the Israel and Palestine of the Vegas bachelorette party.

A couple of minutes after the room pairings email hit my inbox, my cell phone rang, and it was Samantha.

"Do you believe they're pairing us with total strangers?" she said, sounding like a miffed cartoon character.

"I know," I said, numbly. "It's annoying, but hopefully they'll be nice!" I was desperate to put a positive spin on my impending hell.

"I don't know," Samantha said skeptically. "They're probably going to want to party hard, and I'm going to be on a cleanse that weekend." Samantha was always trying something extreme in an attempt to lose weight. "This new doctor I'm seeing has me only drinking green shakes. Do you think they'll have a fridge in our room? I need to have a shake every two hours, and it has to be kept cold."

Samantha was on a roll. "By the way, we should totally take your Prius to save on gas money. Oh, and can I drive? I get carsick easily if I'm not driving."

Lucky. Me.

That fateful Friday morning, I met up with the LA girls and we all caravaned to Vegas, with Samantha sipping on a green shake, driving my Prius with the AC blasting.

Upon our arrival at the hotel (which was called The Hotel—fuck off), we were greeted by a group of blow-up penises being flung about by a gaggle of giddy sorority sisters. The garish, overly marbled lobby echoed with shouts of "Wheeeeeee, this is going to be so much fun!" and "Let's get drunk!"

Up in our room, Samantha and I met the two sorority sisters who were to be our roommates for the weekend. They were very nice, but Samantha wasn't having it.

"Did you see how that one girl looked at me when I asked if I could empty out the mini bar?" Samantha hiss-whispered, sounding like an angry cartoon character as she pulled me into the bathroom and closed the door. "Like, dagger eyes! But it's, like, how am I supposed to fit my shakes on top of the Jim Beam?!" She scoffed. "Ugh, *Kaaate,* you can't leave my side this whole trip! I *need* you!"

I nodded and contemplated getting blackout drunk through a penis straw.

The rest of the weekend was a whirlwind of penis everything, green shakes, drunk girls, green shakes, male strippers, green shakes, and Samantha and I in our shared double bed.

On the last night of the trip, the head sister in charge had arranged a giant dinner with a set menu. We had all paid for it already as part of the lump sum that included our rooms, the limo to the strip club, and so on. Samantha was determined to get her money's worth.

"I already got my doctor's permission to have this one meal here," she told me at the restaurant banquet table, where I was sitting across from her because, well, she ordered me to. "But I need to order off the regular menu because I can't eat any of these set options," she said, perusing the menu that the restaurant had printed with

Bea's name at the top. The sorority sister who had arranged the whole dinner was within earshot and marched over to Samantha.

Here we go.

"You have to order off the set menu," she said, peering down at Samantha in her skintight tube dress. "They'll charge us extra if you order off the regular menu, and everything is already paid for."

I wanted to tell the sister that it probably wasn't the best idea to mess with a hungry girl who had been drinking nothing but green sludge for two days, but I bit my tongue. I was spent. I hate Vegas.

Samantha glared at the sister, then flagged down the waiter and ordered plain white fish with *no oil* and a side of steamed spinach with *no oil* and ate the whole thing with a penis fork.

The next morning was Sunday, which meant it was time to get the *fuck* out of Vegas. Samantha and I packed up and headed down to meet the caravan, and just as we walked out of The Hotel doors, we saw the rest of the LA girls drive off without us, even though we had planned to caravan again with some of the girls switching cars at rest stops so we could continue socializing to the bitter end.

"I need to get back for a wardrobe fitting!" Bea yelled out the car window as they peeled out of the parking lot. I guess they couldn't take the heat, or the green shakes.

"That is so rude!" Samantha said, stomping her foot, defiantly cartoonish as I asked the valet to bring up my car. "This diet isn't working. Let's stop at In-N-Out Burger on the way home," she said, and grabbed my keys. "I'm driving."

#WhyNot **If you have to be chained to an awkward situation, at least look good doing it with this DIY Vintage Rhinestone Body Chain.**

DIY Vintage
Rhinestone Body Chain

PREP IT

2 chains, in different lengths

Wire cutters

Vintage rhinestone bracelet, belt, or necklace

4 large jump rings

2 pairs of pliers

1 jewelry clasp

DO IT!

1. Size the chain you want to use around your neck and cut it with the wire cutters (I used a 20-inch chain).

2. Cut the clasp off the rhinestone bracelet or cut a 6-inch piece from a rhinestone belt or necklace.

3. From the other chain, cut a long piece to fit around your waist and up to the back of your neck, leaving a little slack for a sexy drape (I used a 58-inch piece of chain).

4. Open the jump rings using two pairs of pliers and pass them through the center link of each chain. Use the jump rings to attach the center of the neck chain and waist chain to opposite ends of the rhinestone piece. Close the jump rings with the pliers.

5. Attach each end of the long body chain to each end of the neck chain with jump rings and add the clasp to the jump ring on the right side.

6. Wear by putting your arms through the chain pieces on either side of the rhinestone center divider and clasping the neck chain around your neck. Style your body chain over a tight dress or under a top with a low neckline.

DO IT Elsewhere! If body chains aren't your thing, make a necklace using a piece of an old rhinestone bracelet and leave off the waist chain.

Chapter 45
AUNT CRAY-CRAY

The closest I ever got to being arrested was by my aunt. Joey and I came out to my Prius parked on the street to find my aunt and five cop cars surrounding my unassuming eco-mobile.

"It's them!" She pointed at us as if we'd just robbed a bank.

The cop looked at us, and then back at her, probably finally cluing in to her insanity. He sighed and walked toward us.

"I'm going to have to confiscate your parking permit," he said, bored, indicating the parking placard hanging from my rearview mirror that allowed me to park ticket free on this residential Los Angeles street.

"Of course," Joey said, nodding, and handed him the permit from inside the car. "Just so you know, this is a family issue."

The cop nodded knowingly, turned around, and said to the gaggle of awaiting po-pos, "We're good. Let's get out of here."

My aunt looked disappointed that we weren't in cuffs. She huffed a sigh of deep-seated discontent and marched back to the house that my mom owned and she lived in, head held high in the workout clothes that she wore all day, every day. Her sons and a group of their friends, who had gathered to watch the drama unfold, marched behind her, clutching their handheld video-game appendages. Her sons had been transfixed by those electronic boxes for most of their lives, I'm assuming to avoid the hell that was their mother.

The backstory is—well, it's simple—my aunt is a crazy person. My mom owned a house that she let my aunt and her three kids live in while my aunt got back on her feet after her divorce. Ten years later . . . my aunt still lived there. We all shared the parking passes for the neighborhood until one day, when she went cray.

She wasn't always an angry wacko. This aunt—let's call her Aunt Cray-Cray—was very cute as a youngster. She always garnered male attention with ease, and after divorcing her gay husband, she got right back into having boyfriends, although the quality of human dropped considerably.

After a string of total winners, and by winners I mean losers, including a C-list actor who was a drunk and married, and a cop who coached her on how to pass a lie detector test in between sexcapades, she had settled on the worst yet: a litigation lawyer with rage issues.

One day, Joey and I stopped by the house to find that the litigator had parked his car blocking the large driveway. Joey went up to the house to knock on the door and the guy went rogue. He yelled at Joey in front of my kid cousins to the point that Joey said, "Maybe we should take this outside, away from the kids," as he feared the guy might punch him or, worse, cause permanent psychological damage to my cousins. Litigator Man eventually stormed out and moved his car, glaring at us the whole time.

He was literally the worst. And then he died.

No, I'm serious. Months later, my mom was trying to sell the house, because God knows she was losing money letting her sister live there for a *verrry* reduced rent. Aunt Cray-Cray took great offense that my mom was finally retracting her enabling and started a case against her, which included trying to get me arrested for using the parking permit and claiming "tenant rights" and refusing to move. The legalese in the letters she kept spewing were obviously being written by somebody who knew their way around legal threats, probably the angry litigator.

The war raged on for months, with Cray-Cray refusing to move out, until one day the letters stopped. My mom called me and said, "The litigator died."

"What?" I exclaimed. "How?"

"He went to the beach and dove into the ocean and misjudged the water level," she said. "He broke his neck!"

"Holy shit!" I couldn't believe it.

"Yeah, Cray-Cray just sent a letter saying that she'd move if I gave her eighty thousand dollars," my mom said proudly.

I rolled my eyes on the other end of the phone. "What a bargain."

#WhyNot **My aunt wanted me in chains, and I wanted her in a straitjacket. Here are two ways to embellish the backs of your tired clothes with ties and chains.**

DIY Chain Dress and Back That Bow Up Sweater

Chain Dress

PREP IT

Various chains—large, lightweight chains can be found in the trim section at the fabric store

A dress with a scoop back

Wire cutter

Thread, to match your dress

Needle

DO IT!

1. Plan the layout of the chains on the back of the dress. I started about 3 inches down from the shoulder seam with my thickest chain. Trim them as needed. Tip: You may want to try on the dress to size your chain lengths to make sure there's enough slack for your desired swag.

2. Thread the needle. Doubling the thread and tying a knot at the end helps to make it stronger. Stitch one end of your first piece of chain to the seam at the back of the dress by simply looping the needle through the chain link and through the fabric of the dress until the chain is securely attached. Tie off the thread and cut.

3. Repeat on the opposite side of the dress with the other end of the chain.

4. Repeat steps 2 and 3, using as many pieces of chain as you like. Try on your dress again halfway through to make sure you like how the chains are hanging.

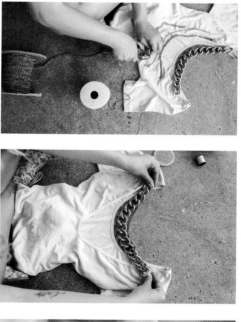

Back That Bow Up Sweater

PREP IT

Sweater

Scissors

Iron-on hem tape

Iron and ironing board

Washcloth

Hot glue gun and fabric glue sticks

12 pieces of ribbon

DO IT!

1. Cut the back of the sweater down the middle.

2. Hem the cut sides by creating an inch-wide fold toward the inside of the sweater and sandwiching a piece of iron-on hem tape between the fold. Iron the hem with a hot iron. Tip: Sometimes it helps to use a moist washcloth to intensify the seal, but check the hem tape package and sweater fabric first to avoid scorching.

3. Cut the ribbon strips to about 12 inches each, using an angled cut to prevent fraying. I used 12 pieces of ribbon to make 6 bows.

4. Plan the layout of the ribbons down the back of your sweater, making sure they're evenly spaced all the way down, and hot-glue the ribbons to the inside of the hemmed sweater opening to secure.

5. Tie the bows and back that bow up!

Chapter 46

THERAPY IN THE CITY

My parents got divorced between the second and third seasons of *Sex and the City*.

I was seventeen and so excited because I had just gotten the opportunity to intern on the set of my favorite television show. Watching *Sex and the City* was my introduction to adult relationships, and I couldn't wait to live like Carrie Bradshaw rather than cry every day about my parents' failed marriage.

My parents told us they were getting divorced in May, and in July I left LA for New York City to stay with my grandma and work for the show that was quickly becoming a social movement of empowered women in beautiful shoes.

I started out working in the production offices at Silver Cup studios, the giant soundstage in Queens where they housed all the sets used on the show. I quickly learned the production office was as far away from the action as you could get on a show. Instead of being on-set, around hundreds of pairs of designer shoes and hot actors, as I had imagined, I was surrounded by copy machines, crabby producers, and stacks of scripts. After the first week of eating too many bagels and copying hundreds of script pages, I asked if I could assist in Patricia Field's costume department, since I was hoping to become a fashion designer. I'd like to think it was the sketches that I presented to the producers that got me moved, but realistically it happened because my dad, the CEO of HBO, was basically everyone's boss.

However I got there, I had made it to the land of Manolos! I spent the days helping in the giant costume department room, lusting after all of Carrie's clothes and accessories. The four "girls," as we all called them, Sarah Jessica Parker, Cynthia Nixon, Kim Cattrall, and Kristin Davis (Carrie, Miranda, Samantha, and Charlotte) would come in for fittings of the amazing ensembles that Patricia styled. I eagerly stood at the ready to steam clothes, change out shoes, and snap Polaroids of the approved looks. I assisted Patricia and her partner, Rebecca, on their errands to shop for extravagant clothes and killer shoes for the upcoming episodes. Rebecca drove Patricia's tiny, bubble-shaped vintage car with Patricia chain-smoking in the passenger seat and me crammed in the backseat, loving life. We'd shop anywhere from Jimmy Choo to tiny vintage stores in the Village, every store treating them like style royalty, while I carried all the outfits and took notes.

I had proved myself enthusiastically willing to work the fourteen-hour days, so for the last two weeks of my internship I was promoted to be a set production assistant (PA). I was given my very own walkie-talkie headset and told to do everything from bringing Kim Cattrall her organic applesauce to digging the cream cheese out of the trash can for John Corbett (Aiden, to all of us *SATC* fans) to keeping people on the sidewalks of NYC from ruining the girls' walk and talk scenes.

I was around all of the cast members, and they were all really nice, but my favorite was SJP. Sarah Jessica Parker was so kind to me on-set. I had met her a couple of times before at HBO parties with my dad, so the first time I saw her in the hallway during the first week of my internship, she hugged me and said, "I'm so glad you're here, Kate! It's going to be so fun having you around!"

Entranced by her acknowledgment, I blushed and thanked her. Then she looked straight in my eyes with a clear, knowing gaze and said, "I'm so sorry to hear about your parents." She squeezed my hand.

I floated through the rest of the day feeling like the fifth girl of *Sex and the City*. I was ready to sit down at the coffee shop with Carrie, Miranda, Samantha, and Charlotte and talk about all our problems.

As the summer wore on and my days in NYC were numbered, I started to prepare myself to return to the land of divorce. Sarah Jessica had become like, the world's most fashionable therapist. She would spend time between scenes talking with me about how I was coping and lending advice and understanding, since she had been through her own parents' divorce as a kid. She'd brush off the assistant director's request for her to get back to the scene and would put her tiny, Pilates-toned arms around me and give me a big hug and tell me I was going to be okay when tears sprung in my eyes.

Carrie Bradshaw went on to become an iconic female figure for our generation, and for a few moments, in the summer of 2000, she was my friend.

#WhyNot **Carrie Bradshaw's therapy was always a quirky pair of shoes; treat yourself with these statement DIY Gecko Shoes.**

DIY Gold Gecko Shoes

PREP IT

Drop cloth or scrap cardboard

Gold spray paint

Plastic geckos (rubber doesn't work
well with spray paint)

Shoes with a thick heel or wedge

Masking tape

Strong glue, like E6000 or 3M Scotch Super
Strength Adhesive

DO IT!

1. Outside on a drop cloth or scrap
cardboard, spray paint the plastic
geckos gold and let them dry completely.

2. Carefully glue a golden gecko to each heel of your shoes and use small pieces of masking tape to hold them in place as they dry. Tip: If the tape takes off any paint after the geckos are secured to the heel, touch them up using a small paint brush and gold paint, or add gold glitter using a little Mod Podge glue!

DO IT Elsewhere! Glue a gold spray-painted reptile tail to the top of a cork to make a decorative wine stopper!

Chapter 47
ONE FLEW INTO THE CUCKOO'S NEST

I have two kids, and part of any new relationship is making sure their new dad is ready to step up to the plate . . . and scoop their litter. Yeah, my kids are cats. I'm a crazy cat lady.

My romance with Joey blossomed on opposite coasts of the U.S.A. He lived in Boston and I lived in LA and we tried to visit each other as much as possible. I'd meet him on tour and stay with him in Boston, or he'd come to my apartment in LA. Thankfully, he had a lot of frequent flyer miles racked up from traveling around the world with his band.

He didn't start out as a cat guy, but like a true Prince Charming, he became infatuated with me and my pussies.

I bought the cats when I was a sophomore in college—yeah, I'm the devil, I didn't rescue them! But I was young and I didn't yet know the rules. I've kept the fact that my cats aren't rescued as a deep, dark secret for so many years . . . it's so nice to finally come clean!

I got these particular cats because they're Ragdolls. I wanted a breed of cat that was the most friendly, affectionate, and cuddly. They actually go limp like floppy dolls when you hold them, which sounds creepy but is fucking adorable. I've had my fluffballs, Roxanne and Winston, for twelve years now. They're my BFFs, and when they die, I'll have to go to intense grief counseling.

So yeah, I love my cats, and thankfully, so does Joey.

During the second year of our long-distance relationship, Joey had just left to go back to Boston to record some new music with the band when I noticed that Winston, my little boy cat, couldn't pee! Like, he'd keep going to the litter box, squat, and nothing would come out!

I freaked out. I'm kind of a drama queen, especially when it comes to my four-legged children. I drove Winston to the vet, sobbing to Joey on the phone (hands-free, of course), my eyes clouded with tears.

"What if he explodes!?" I cried. "He can't get the pee out!"

"I'm sure he'll be fine," Joey consoled me as he stepped out of the recording studio in Boston to talk me off my ledge. "Let's see what the vet says. Call me as soon as you hear from him, and give Winston a pat for me."

Awwww, so cute, right? But I couldn't focus on how lovely Joey was with Winston cry-meowing in the cat carrier in my backseat.

At the vet they told me that Winston had cystitis, which is when crystals form in the bladder and cause a blockage. They would have to catheterize his miniature penis, and hopefully that would release the blockage.

"If that doesn't work, we're going to have to cut off his penis," said the vet. "This will give him a bigger hole for the urine to pass."

I was beside myself. I called Joey.

"They have to cut off his penis!!" I wailed as I defaulted to the worst-case scenario.

"What?" Joey said. I could hear the wail of a guitar in the background.

"Winston is going to be a tranny cat!" I hollered. The other people in the waiting room were looking at me with alarm.

"They have to stick a tube up his little sandpaper penis," I whispered through tears. "I feel so bad for him! I want to be there for him during his transition. I wonder if there are books on this? Do we need to give him a more gender-neutral name?" I was spiraling.

Joey tried to calm me down, but I was at my wit's end.

I had to leave Winston there overnight, so I finally went home. I was allowed to call in to the vet to get reports on how he was doing, which I did, like, every thirty minutes.

While I was on my ten P.M. call, my phone beeped with a text message. It was from Joey and it read: *Getting on a plane to come to LA to be with you and da kitties.*

Joey had just left for Boston twenty-four hours prior, and now he was getting back on a plane to be with me in my hour of need.

You don't have to do that! I texted back.

He responded: *I want to! It just sucks because we're recording, so I can only stay for twelve hours.*

At that moment, I knew this was the guy I had to be with for the rest of my life. I mean, what other dude would fly across the country for half a day to emotionally rescue a crazy girl and her cat!?

Thankfully, Winston got to keep his penis and Joey has become a permanent member of our furry family.

Joey, during one of his visits from Boston, making Winston (and me) feel better

#WhyNot **Some might call me cuckoo, but Joey calls me Boo-Boo. Keep your crazy in a box with this DIY Deconstructed Cuckoo Clock.**

DIY Deconstructed Cuckoo Clock

PREP IT

Painter's tape

Shoe box lid (I kept mine white, but you can paint yours any color)

Acrylic paint in the color of your choice

Paintbrush

Lightweight chain

Wire cutters

2 old keys

Center pendulum charm
(I used a moon-shaped brooch)

2 pairs of pliers

3 open jump rings

Battery-operated clock movement

Decorative cuckoo bird

Hot glue gun and glue sticks

Hammer and nail, for hanging

DO IT!

2. Cut three lengths of chain for the keys and pendulum charm (I chose to make the center pendulum piece shorter). Attach the keys and charm to the chains using the pliers to open and close the jump rings.

1. Tape off a very simple house shape on the front of the shoe box lid, essentially a triangle on top of a rectangle, and paint within the tape lines using your acrylic paint color (I mixed purple and white to get a lavender shade). Let dry.

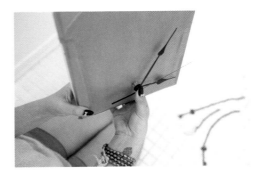

3. Decide where you want the clock arms to go on the house and poke a hole with the wire cutters to push the threaded clock movement shaft through, securing the clock body on the underside of the shoe box lid and the clock hands in front. Don't worry if the clock hands extend beyond the edges of the shoe box—it will still work! But do keep in mind where you plan to put the bird, so that it isn't hit by the clock hands.

4. Poke three holes in the bottom lip of your shoe box and feed the chains of your keys and pendulum charms through. Secure them on the underside with some hot glue.

5. Carefully remove the painter's tape to reveal the house shape. Hot-glue the decorative cuckoo bird near the pointed peak. Hang the finished clock on your wall with a nail!

DO IT Elsewhere! Update an old hat with a decorative cuckoo bird hatband!

Chapter 48

EARTHQUAKES AND BREAST BUDS

When your boobs start to come in, they start as these little breast buds—tiny cherry pit–looking things behind your nipple that are so darn sore. Being ten years old and dealing with this disruptive force on my flat chest was keeping me up at night.

I lived in a cul-de-sac around the corner from our school in Northridge, California. On a particularly warm January night, I was fitfully tossing in bed, trying to cool myself down and get more comfortable. I took off my shirt and threw it on the floor next to my bed so I could let my swollen nuggets breathe.

I was finally sleeping soundly and cool when something else erupted. At 4:31 A.M., I awoke in the epicenter of one of the largest earthquakes in United States history. The Northridge earthquake registered at 6.7 on the Richter scale, and being in the dead center felt like the world was ending.

My dad ran into the room and grabbed me out of bed, and we ducked in the doorway. He had been hit in the leg by a flying side table and was bleeding, but other than that we were unscathed. My mom joined us seconds later, holding my three-year-old sister, Tess. The jostling was so intense that you couldn't stand up, and it sounded like a train was going straight through the center of our house.

After what seemed like forever, the loud rumbling suddenly stopped and the house creaked back to an eerie stillness. The house was pitch-black. All of the electricity and streetlights had gone out, and the only remaining glint of light was my battery-operated nightlight dimly illuminating the floor of my bedroom. I peered in and saw that all of the contents of my shelves had fallen to the floor. My books, dolls, and—oh, no—my crystal collection had become a jumbled stew. The week before I had carefully styled my precious crystal collection of natural geodes, polished quartz, and mica on the shelves above my desk, and now they were in a mess on the floor.

My parents did a quick survey. "Everyone okay?"

"Yeah. Fine," I said, pissed about my crystals. I didn't realize how close we'd all come to being a family of pancakes.

"What about Megan?" my mom asked, referring to our twenty-two-year-old live-in nanny, who stayed in the guest bedroom at the other end of our long house.

My parents had hired Megan to look after us while they worked. The unconventional part was that my parents let Megan have her boyfriend Steve sleep over. Steve was an undertaker who did special effects makeup on dead accident victims to cover the gory wounds that had killed them so they could have an open-casket funeral. The whole thing freaked me out, and I was wary of touching things that Steve had touched because I thought he had dead people germs. I couldn't believe Megan actually wanted to have sleepovers with him! Eww.

My parents yelled down the long hallway to Megan, hoping she was alive—and not in need of Steve's reconstructive services!

"I'm okay!" yelled back a muffled voice. "The bookshelf fell on the bed and almost crushed Steve . . . but we're both okay."

Steve was still a dead makeup artist walking.

"Meet us in front of the house," my mom yelled. We all made our way through the rubble to the front door.

Outside, I remembered I was topless. I insecurely crossed my arms over my chest so that Steve and our neighbors, who were all gathering in the cul-de-sac, couldn't see my budding womanhood. My dad saw that I was topless and embarrassed and took off his raggedy sleep shirt to give to me, now showing off his hairy man-boobs to the neighborhood.

Huddled together on the pavement, we waited out a couple more aftershocks, and when the sun was dawning enough for us to see inside, we went back in to assess the damage.

It was chaos! Every single freestanding thing had fallen. Tables, chairs, art, bookshelves—even a nine-foot-tall antique armoire that my parents got from a Mexico salvage yard had fallen over and slid across the hardwood floor. The marble mantelpiece over the fireplace had fallen four feet off the wall and lay cracked in half on the rug. The worst part was that my mom had been on a bulk health-food buying spree earlier that month and had stocked up on applesauce, sauerkraut, prune juice, and pickled radishes, all of which had toppled out of the cabinet and broken on the tile floor of our kitchen, leaving a six-inch-deep slop of organic disgustingness.

My parents, Steve, and Megan began cleaning up while Tess and I went in search of my crystals and our two cats. I hoped they were alive—I didn't know if Steve's mortician services extended to animals.

#WhyNot **When the earth splits, stuff some crystals in it and make a DIY Crystal-Inlaid Side Table.**

DIY Crystal-Inlaid Side Table

PREP IT

Wood stump (I raided mine from my neighbor's tree trimmings; find them at lumber yards or landscaping supply stores)

Sandpaper (optional)

Wood chisel

Hammer

Crystals

2 to 4 boxes of epoxy resin, depending on the size of the stump

Disposable container and stir stick, to mix your epoxy

Polycrylic (seals and keeps out wood critters)

3-inch-wide paintbrush

Drill

Table legs and screws (optional; if your stump is thin and you want to add height)

DO IT!

1. Wood stumps that have been cut with a mechanical saw usually have smooth faces, so pick the side of the stump you want to be the top of the table. You may want to sand down some of the uneven ridges—I chose to leave them for an organic look. If you have a thick stump that won't need legs to make it the right height for a side table to a chair or couch, make sure it's stable. If you have a thinner slice of wood, like mine, make sure the legs will be able to attach evenly to the underside after you're done with the crystal inlay.

2. Using a wood chisel and hammer, carve out areas of the wood stump where you want to inlay the crystals. If you want them to lie flush with the rest of the wood, chisel a deeper inset. Tip: Chiseling is easy—just hammer the end of the chisel handle to chip out pieces of wood. Don't worry about making it perfect. Practice your technique on a scrap piece of wood, if you like.

3. Fill in the chiseled areas with crystals, packing them as densely as possible.

4. Follow the instructions on the box to stir together the epoxy resin. This usually involves heating up the two bottles in warm water and stirring equal parts together for around 4 minutes. Stir the resin slowly to avoid air bubbles.

5. Slowly pour the resin mixture over your crystal insets (up to you if you want to leave the crystals peeking out of the resin or cover them completely). For a glossier look, add a thin layer of epoxy over the wood top.

(Don't worry if a little drips down the sides—you can wipe it off or let it cure as glossy drips.) Tip: Use a small propane torch to pop any bubbles that form and achieve a high shine while the resin is still wet. I didn't use a torch and instead used my resin stir stick to pop and smooth any bubbles that rose from the spaces in the crystals after the initial pour.

6. Let the resin cure for 3 full days in a still, dust-free area.

7. If you haven't covered it in a coat of resin, seal the wood on all sides with a painted coat or two of polycrylic.

8. Use the drill to screw the table legs to the underside of the stump (I used 3 hairpin style legs).

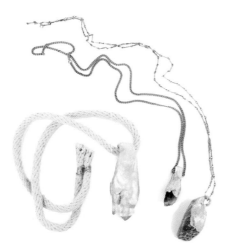

DO IT Elsewhere! Use baked polymer clay to make a setting for a crystal necklace pendant. Paint the clay with metallic acrylic paint and hang on a chain or rope!

Chapter 49
I BARF ON VACATION

I barf on vacation. It's gotten to the point where I've had food poisoning or some kind of stomach bug so many times that it's beyond coincidence; I'm officially allergic to travel.

It didn't used to happen. The only time I had a stomach issue while away from home was when I was twelve and my family visited Venice, Italy. We stayed in the gorgeous Hotel Cipriani, which had a saltwater swimming pool and amazing restaurants. I got a gas bubble and was so nervous about it that my stomach spasmed, so my parents sent for a doctor. This hot Italian man came to our room with a little black bag and gave me a shot in my butt cheek. My mom was so enamored with his looks that only after he'd stuck me did she think to ask what the foreign doctor was administering to her daughter via hypodermic needle.

Me, pre-barf-browsing an outdoor market in Vietnam

"Muscle relaxer," was his response.

To which I farted and fell asleep.

It's only now, as an adult, that I consistently get sick on pretty much every trip I take. I've since barfed all over the world.

There was the first time I visited Joey's parents in Indiana, where I got sick off some organic raspberries and spent the first night in their guest bathroom evacuating Whole Foods' finest. Unfortunately, the bathroom backed up against Joey's parents' bedroom, so in the morning his mom said she'd heard me retching all night. I'd hardly gotten to know them, but they already knew how many times I'd had diarrhea.

The next incident happened in Vietnam. Joey was there with the Click Five to headline a charity concert to raise awareness against human trafficking. We went to Ho Chi Minh City for a couple of days before the concert was to take place. The nonprofit put the band up in the InterContinental hotel, where each band member had his own suite. It was amazing! The day of the concert, Joey and I went to visit a local Vietnamese family we had met, and they cooked us a feast. To drink, they served iced tea made from the tap water that I had been avoiding up to that point, but out of politeness, I imbibed. Sure enough, on the moped ride back to get ready for the show, my stomach began to churn. I tried to ignore it because I was *not* going to miss Joey playing for twenty thousand people that night—the entire reason we'd flown across the Pacific to this glorious country.

Alas, twenty minutes before we were supposed to leave with the band to go to the giant arena, I barfed, and shit, and barfed again.

Joey felt so bad, but of course he had to go, because what's a rock band without a drummer!? I lay on the floor of the giant bathroom in the giant empty suite and kept a-barfin'. Eventually I called down to the front desk to tell them I was probably going to die. They offered to send a doctor.

The doctor showed up with his helper. They were two Vietnamese men, the doctor in white scrubs and the helper in navy blue. They were both as short as I am (five-foot even) and didn't speak any English. I lay down on the bed and the doctor gave me disgusting green powdered electrolytes to drink and a shot in my arm. I asked him what was in the syringe and feebly tried to inspect to see if it was sterile. He didn't understand my question but nodded and smiled. I was desperate and I offered him my arm. Moments later my heart was racing, and I thought I was officially dying. *Great, I'm going to die of dehydration and a heart attack in 'Nam!* I thought. My dad had escaped the draft but I would succumb to the tap water. I was so anxious that I called down to the front desk and put them on speakerphone so they could translate to the doctor that I thought I was dying of a heart attack. The front desk person then translated to me that Doctor Vietnam had given me an antinausea medicine that sometimes can cause heart palpitations, and I should just take deep breaths to calm down.

Joey came back to the hotel several hours later, all sweaty from playing drums for twenty thousand people, and I was panting in my pajamas on the king-size bed with an electrolyte milk mustache. Not. Cute.

The next time I barfed on vacation was when Joey took me to an eco-resort in Mexico for my twenty-ninth birthday. "Eco" meant eco-friendly, which meant that the open-air oceanfront hut we stayed in had mosquito netting around the bed (to protect from the giant bugs) and partial walls (even in the bathroom), and you had to put your toilet paper in the trash can—not down the toilet. It was beautiful but rustic, and the worst place to get food poisoning. The local farmers made raw chocolate from cacao plants grown on the mountains above. It was delicious and I promptly ate three giant balls of the raw goodness. It was pure bliss until my intestines were like, "*No me gustan!*"

That night, the evacuation commenced. Having food poisoning while sleeping inside a mosquito net is the worst thing ever. I had to untuck it every time I got up to run to the bathroom. I got tangled many times on my mad dash and almost impaled myself on the rugged wood bedpost. Once in the bathroom, the half walls did nothing to block out my heaving and sharting noises, with poor Joey in the bed beyond. I also had to throw my cacao-smeared toilet remnants in the trash can! *Not. Cute.*

My barfing came full circle when I visited Italy again as an adult. My mom was hosting Joey's family for a few days at the Tuscan villa she rented. We all made a gorgeous pasta dinner that everyone ate and enjoyed on the beautiful patio, overlooking the adjacent vineyard. Later that night, I was the only one on my hands and knees admiring the Italian toilet as my *penne alla checca* swirled its way to the Venetian canals. I finally lulled myself to sleep on the blue-and-white-tiled bathroom floor, longing for that dreamy Venetian doctor, his black bag, and his magical syringe.

I have big plans to travel the world in my lifetime. I advise you all to invest in Pepto-Bismol stock.

#WhyNot **This stylish DIY Exotic Head Wrap is quick and easy for laid-back chic while on an exotic vacation—and it will keep your hair out of the toilet when you accidentally drink the tap water.**

DIY Exotic Head Wrap

PREP IT

Hair elastic

Long scarf

DO IT!

1. Pull all your hair into a ponytail on the top of your head where you want the knot of your scarf to sit and secure it with an elastic. If you have short hair, skip this step!

2. Place the center of the scarf at the nape of your neck and crisscross the two lengths around at your forehead, encasing your ponytail in the center, the way you would if you were wrapping your hair in a towel.

3. Keep twisting the scarf until the entire length is in one big twist, then coil it into a bun and tuck the end securely at the base of your coil. The length of your ponytail that's wrapped in the twist will help to anchor your knot. Add some sunglasses and earrings to complete the look!

DO IT Elsewhere! Use a printed square scarf to elegantly wrap your to-go lunch or a gift!

Chapter 50

GET ME TO THE COURT ON TIME

I never wanted to get married. It just didn't excite me. I always knew I wanted to find a mate and have a family, but the whole ring, white dress, and wedding stress made me queasy. As much as I like party dresses, I never fantasized about my wedding day. The institution of marriage seemed an archaic one, built during the days of tribes and dowries. I am not a possession to be "given away," nor did I want to force people to choose between the fish or the steak. Plus, growing up in Hollywood, marriage is kind of a joke. No one stays married, so the whole thing just seemed pointless.

When I met Joey, a good ol' Indiana boy, we fell madly in love and immediately imagined turning into wrinkly old cuties together, but he couldn't believe that I didn't want to get married. He was raised in a world where, duh, that's just what you do! You find a career, meet a girl, get married, have kids, stay married, get a timeshare in Florida, eat fried pickles, and then die of cardiovascular complications . . . who wouldn't want that!?

Me.

Riding across the country on Joey's tour bus, we'd spend the long drives lying together in his bunk, finding out every last detail about each other and what we wanted for our futures. He told me how he imagined riding into his wedding on a donkey. Either that or swinging in on a flying trapeze—he hadn't decided yet, but he knew it was going to be a big show.

I loved his weirdness, but I methodically explained my feminist stance. "Marriage is founded on religious beliefs that I just don't have!" I said.

"Yeah, but it's relationship security," Joey insisted. "It makes it harder to leave."

"Oh, so a prisoner is what you want?" I joked, poking his smiling cheek, neither of us taking it too seriously.

I'd then highlight that it is a false sense of security that puts more pressure on a relationship and ultimately dooms something that should be magical.

"What about our future kids?" he cajoled.

"Bastard children are just as cute as legitimate children," I said, then hugged him. "I can't wait to have some little bastards with you!"

He shut me up with a kiss and a playful ass slap, and we agreed to figure it out down the road.

Six years later, Joey and I, still madly in love, running a successful business together, and enjoying an even more successful relationship, believed that everything was perfect. Joey's always been good at putting himself in other people's shoes. He totally understood where I was coming from on the marriage thing and loved me for my independent way of questioning tradition. We both blissfully dove willingly into the world of lifelong committed unmarried-ness.

We are now married.

One day we walked into our accountant's office, chests puffed out, proud of our blissful dissentience from the norm.

"We're ready to buy a house!" I exclaimed.

"Cool," she said. "You guys should really get married. You're wasting money on taxes, health insurance, and blah blah blah." She didn't actually say blah blah blah, but that's what it sounds like to me any time someone starts talking about math and taxes.

Joey later explained her point to me more poetically. The world was punishing us for not being married. We would save money *and* be able to pull the plug on each other if we were ever facing imminent death.

"Fuck it, let's get married," I said, romantically, knowing that whatever my feminist persuasions, I always wanted Joey to be my In Case of Emergency. "But don't tell *anyone*!"

It was December, and we decided there was no point in putting it off until the next year, because we might as well start receiving all those annoying tax benefits as soon as possible. So Joey and I hopped in the car and went to the courthouse to get the marriage license, which felt a lot like paying a traffic ticket. We thought that was all we had to do until the lady behind the glass asked, "When are you having your ceremony?"

"We're not having a ceremony," Joey replied.

"You need to have the union officiated for it to count," she said, looking bored. "The only appointment we have before 2014 is tomorrow at one forty-five P.M. at the East LA courthouse."

Joey looked at me and grinned. "We'll take it!" I immediately got nauseous.

The next day was a Thursday, and I wore a cat print T-shirt and a black tutu—there was nothing white or virginal about my outfit. Joey wore jeans. We left our office, telling our employees we were going to a lunch meeting, and drove the LA freeways to a gritty area of East LA.

We sat outside in the courtyard of the single-level courthouse, waiting to be called in. There were a few gay couples who got married before us. I liked seeing the gay guys and lesbians going in and out of the room; it made the whole institution I was about to enter feel a little more inclusive.

Then there she was. Our black-robed officiant, Deputy Maria Ortiz, a rotund Hispanic lady with crimped curls and drawn-on eyebrows, beckoning us into the room.

The "wedding" room looked as if it could have easily housed public executions. It was small, with linoleum floors, fluorescent lighting, and plastic chairs lined up on one wall. In the center of the room was a gazebo arbor thing, the kind you'd paint white and put in an English garden—only this one was left its drab wood color and had fake red flowers draped all over it. It was hideous.

Deputy Maria had us stand before her. "Do you have any rings?" she asked. We shook our heads no. I looked for the nearest exit.

"That's okay," she said, smiling kindly. "Do you have any vows?" We shook our heads no. I was getting queasy.

"Okay." She laughed. "Then let's just do this thing." I will forever love Deputy Maria Ortiz.

She married us. Just like that, we were *hasbeeend* and *weef*—I still can't say those words. Fortunately for me, Deputy Maria had some trouble saying words as well. Our white-kid names were throwing her off, and that day Kate Alber-sheet and Jo-el Zeerer got married in her courtroom. I'm sort of banking on that as my out if I ever need one.

Hopefully that won't ever happen because I love Joey so crazy much and want to be with him forever, and I'm sure the divorce would take place in that same hideous room.

#WhyNot **Ditch the dress and rock a tutu with this no-fuss DIY No-Sew Tutu.**

DIY No-Sew Tutu

PREP IT

3 yards fine tulle

3 yards stiff tulle

2 yards satin taffeta

2 yards velvet ribbon

Scissors

DO IT!

1. Cut around 40—depending on the size of your waist—hand-width strips of tulle and satin taffeta along the width of the bolt (usually the width of a bolt of tulle is 108 inches). Tip: The tulle is easier to cut when it's folded, and the satin taffeta is easier to rip after you make a starter slit with the scissors.

2. The velvet ribbon will be your waistband. Loop-knot strips of tulle and satin taffeta around the ribbon as follows: Fold a strip in half, place the ribbon near the "U" of the fold, pull the two ends of the strip through the "U," and cinch the loop knot tight around the velvet ribbon. Leave enough ribbon free at both ends to be able to tie it closed around your waist.

3. Repeat step 2 with enough strips of tulle and satin taffeta to cover the circumference of your waist. I chose to alternate my three fabric types, using double the amount of tulle to satin taffeta.

4. Tie the tutu around your waist using the length of ribbon to make a bow in the front or back. Trim the skirt strips to the desired length, if needed. The satin taffeta strips will be heavier and hang under the tulle, creating an underskirt of sorts, but you may still want to wear shorts or tights so as not to risk flashing your booty . . . totally up to you!

DO IT Elsewhere! Tutu your tank top by hot-gluing puckered strips of tulle on the underside of each strap!

RESOURCES

CRAFT SUPPLIES AND TOOLS

Amazon

www.amazon.com

Can't say enough good things about Amazon. You can find pretty much anything you might need, with many things being available Prime or Prime Fresh, so your order arrives in a matter of days. Find wood-burning pens, plastic animals, glue, pliers, wire, paint, papier-mâché letters, Ping-Pong balls, hardware, toy soldiers, clock works, pillow inserts, perfume pumps, bags of crystals, décor items, nail art, beauty supplies, and much more.

Etsy

www.etsy.com

Shop this site for cruelty-free feathers, jewelry-making supplies, handmade pom-poms, vintage perfume bottles, doilies, lockets, and much more.

Home Depot

www.homedepot.com

Shop for more heavy-duty tools, supplies and paint, thick rope, spray paint, large paintbrushes, sandpaper, heavy duty screw hooks and more. Home Depot carries the Minwax brand Polycrylic, which is my favorite sealant to paint over furniture DIY projects to give them a lasting finish.

Jo-Ann Fabric and Craft Stores

www.joann.com

Jo-Ann is like Michael's sister; they have a lot of the same stuff but Jo-Ann boasts a large fabric selection. You can find a lot of tools and supplies, and I also love their unfinished wood crates that look great stained or painted any color. They also offer a lot of coupons and free shipping promotions if you shop online.

Lowes

www.lowes.com

Lowes carries many of the same hardware, paint, and tools as Home Depot. They also usually have an extensive landscaping department with plants like cactuses for the DIY Pretty and Prickly Cactus (page 63).

Michael's

www.michaels.com

Michael's is a great place to get inspired if you're not sure what creative project you want to make. I go to Michael's when I need instant craft supplies like glue, paint, frames, unfinished wood items, tools, ribbon, yarn, sewing supplies, jewelry chain, wire, clasps, and more.

Mood Fabrics

www.moodfabrics.com

I shop the Mood store for fabrics, decorative trim, lace, and ribbon for style and home décor projects. They have a giant selection of fabrics and offer international shipping on their website.

Paper Source

www.papersource.com

The best selection of beautiful paper supplies. Some of the patterned backgrounds in this book were large sheets of paper from this store.

HOME DÉCOR, THRIFT STORES, AND FLEA MARKETS

Goodwill

www.goodwill.org

I shop at Goodwill all the time for inexpensive home and style items that I can spruce up with many of the DIY projects found in this book. Look for vintage silver trays, glassware, shirts, skirts, dresses, jackets, jeans, shoes, purses, and hats.

HomeGoods

www.homegoods.com

My favorite place to shop in-store for affordable home accents like mirrors, throw pillows, lamps, baskets, bedding, and decorative accessories.

IKEA

www.ikea.com

Great for basics like picture frames (I like the ones that come with mats), unfinished wood chairs, light cord kits, dressers, headboards, and pedestal tables.

Luna Bazaar

www.lunabazaar.com

My go-to for the largest variety of paper lanterns, light cord kits, bohemian party and seasonal decorations, and even crochet parasols as seen in DIY Big and Beautiful Hair (page 100).

Melrose Trading Post Flea Market

www.melrosetradingpost.org

My favorite flea market in Los Angeles to browse for everything from vintage furniture and home accents to clothes and rhinestone jewelry. The sellers are educated about their wares and the selection is always fresh.

Salvation Army

www.salvationarmyusa.org

I shop the Salvation Army for the same types of items you can get at the Goodwill as well as a larger selection of furniture. Look for chairs to paint and reupholster (like the DIY Pom-Pom Chair, page 67) and glass-top coffee tables to paint (like the DIY Mercury Glass Coffee Table, page 6).

Target

www.target.com

A great one-stop-shop for curtain panels, décor accessories, basic hardware supplies, and inexpensive clothing items to spruce up.

World Market

www.worldmarket.com

Shop for baskets, rustic wood frames, kitchen and tabletop items, crinkle voile cotton curtain panels (as seen in DIY Basket Canopy, page 167), and more.

CLOTHING, SHOES, JEWELRY, AND ACCESSORIES

ASOS

www.asos.com

A great site for dresses, shoes, and everything in between. They also offer petite and plus size options.

BB Dakota

www.bbdakota.com

Comfortable, well-priced clothing items that are great for layering.

eBay

www.ebay.com

I love eBay for fun shoe finds like the bone heel platforms (featured in DIY No-Sew Tutu, page 269). They are usually factory direct, so allow time for shipping.

Finders Keepers, Keepsake, Jagger, The Fifth, and C/meo Collective

us.fashionbunker.com

These are all clothing lines from Australian designers. Many of the outfits in the book, including the cover outfit, feature items from these labels.

H&M

www.hm.com

A huge selection of affordable and on-trend clothing, accessories, and shoes.

Mr. Kate

www.mrkate.com

Duuuh, I can't not mention my own online store! Nearly every piece of jewelry I wore in this book is from the Mr. Kate jewelry line, designed by me!

Nasty Gal

www.nastygal.com

My go-to online source for edgy fashion and Jeffrey Campbell shoes.

Topshop

www.topshop.com

Shop online or in-store for fun and funky clothes, shoes, and accessories. They offer a great petites selection too.

UrbanOG

www.urbanog.com

A wonderful source for affordable clothing and shoes. Shop for funky platforms or simple pumps to spruce up with bows like the DIY Bow Shoes (page 78).

Whitney Eve

www.whitneyeve.com

A clothing line from designer Whitney Port. I love her fun patterns and use of bright colors.

YesStyle

www.yesstyle.com

A Korean fashion website that I love to shop for cute clothing and accessories like babydoll dresses and backpacks with wings!

Zara

www.zara.com

I love Zara. It is a dangerous store and website for me because I always buy something. I love their crisp and chic aesthetic. Their shoes, jackets, hats, and basics are unparalleled.

HAIR, MAKEUP, AND NAILS

Born Pretty

www.bornprettystore.com

A great source for nail art supplies like 3D decorations.

Concrete Minerals

www.concreteminerals.com

100% vegan and cruelty-free makeup. I love their eyeshadows and eyeshadow primer.

Davines

www.davines.com

Wonderful hair shampoos and conditioners. The LOVE Conditioner is my favorite for curly hair. Their Hair Refresher dry shampoo is my absolute fave.

EcoTools

www.ecotools.com

Eco-friendly makeup brushes you can buy at the drugstore.

Jurlique

www.jurlique.com

My favorite, all-natural face cream I use day and night is Jurlique Moisture Replenishing Day Cream.

Lime Crime

www.limecrime.com

I'm obsessed with their Velvetines lip liquid that dries matte. I wear the Suedeberry, Red Velvet, and Pink Velvet on repeat.

Lorac

www.loraccosmetics.com

I love their eyeshadow palettes like the PRO Palette and the coral blush and bronzer in the PRO To Go palette.

MAC Cosmetics

www.maccosmetics.com

The best red lipstick color ever is MAC's Ruby Woo, and I love their matte pink Please Me.

Oribe

www.oribe.com

Luxurious hair products. I love their Aprés Beach Wave and Shine Spray, Dry Texturizing Spray, and Gold Lust Nourishing Hair Oil.

Sally Beauty Supply

www.sallybeauty.com

Shop in store for nail art supplies like the metallic gold tape used in DIY Metallic Tape Nails (page 96).

SensatioNail

www.sensationail.com

The Gel Starter Kit is an easy way to do at-home gel manicures. It comes with a small LED light to cure the gel polish. A clear gel topcoat really helps to seal your 3D nail art decorations for a longer-lasting manicure. You can use other gel polish brands like Gel-ish with the SensatioNail light.

Sephora

www.sephora.com

Kind of can't beat the selection of designer makeup brands at Sephora. I love Bobbi Brown creamy concealer, Givenchy Photo'Perfexion foundation, Too Faced Better Than Sex Mascara, Marc Jacobs Magic Marc'er Precision Pen liquid liner, Make Up For Ever eyeshadows, and Laura Mercier Secret Brightening Powder.

Starlight Nail Supply

www.starlightnail.com

A great selection of gel nail polish, nail art decorations, and more.

The Hair Shop

www.hairpiece.com

My go-to source for clip-in extensions (as seen in DIY Big and Beautiful Hair, page 100). They offer a huge range of hair colors and will let you try them on in-store.

Acknowledgments

This book wouldn't have been possible without the following amazing, incredible, funny, talented, beautiful, good-smelling peeps:

First, a shout-out to Joey Zehr—without your boss business skills, leadership, creativity, editing know-how, humor, and gorgeous physique, this book would not be nearly as pretty and way more scary-diary-of-a-cat-freak. You make our reality a happy and fruitful one. I'm so happy to be on this business/life journey with you. I love chu.

To badass editor Cassie Jones and her right-hand woman, Kara Zauberman, for seeing value in my madness and not censoring my poop jokes. Cassie, you "get it," and I heart you.

To Alison Fargis, the smartest and most elegant book agent, who showed us around this old and glorious world of books. And the rest of the Stonesong ladies.

Fairy mermaid photographer Laura Austin, for being an absolute genius and a pleasure to work with. And to Agatha Borrelli, for connecting us.

Taren Maroun, for being a photo wizard with all the DIY shots.

Elise Mesa, for your DIY skills and unwavering positivity. You made the projects come alive.

Christina Guerra, your fantastic makeup and hair looks made Carl feel so sexy (inside joke), but really Christina is the best artist in the biz.

Diana Dillon, for being a beautifully tattooed outfit curator.

Chaleena Ukositkul, for keeping us productive and cute at the *Mr. Kate* HQ.

Brad Etter, for capturing and celebrating our creative expressions.

To my super smart, funny, and loving dad, for inspiring me to be a hardworking businesswoman with a sense of humor.

To my mom, for always being my champion and liking the book even though I call you a sea cow. I appreciate the creative weirdo gene you've passed on to me.

To Tess, my little toot, for styling the cover photo and making me feel purdy. Thank you for always being my best friend. I love you so much and I'm excited to grow old with you.

To Granny, my female role model in strength, love, and thrift stores. Thank you for reading me all those books.

To the Zehrs, my functional family, I love you.

To my birthday-twin therapist Margaret, who gave me the emotional tools to be a happy bitch.

And finally, to all of you who bought and read this book and still managed to like me! May you keep creating and loving yourself, quirks and all.